seam

shoulder line

Yoke back
neck size 15½
chest size 40

met. gold
#106

red#17/#20
inside

red #17

pink
#20

red
#17 red
#20
(alternate)

straight grain

main sleeve

gabardine - 1⅛ yd.
interfacing 1⅛ yd
white - 1 yd.

style 440 5

red
#17/#20
inside

grain

PUBLISHED BY

RIZZOLI
NEW YORK

300 PARK AVENUE SOUTH
NEW YORK, NY 10010

HILLBILLY HOLLYWOOD

BY *Debby Bull*

HILLBILLY HOLLYWOOD

THE ORIGINS OF COUNTRY & WESTERN STYLE

BY DEBBY BULL

FEATURING THE VINTAGE COSTUME COLLECTION OF MARTY STUART

CIP: 99 076187   ISBN: 0-8478-2278

First published in the United States of America in 2000 by

Rizzoli International Publications, Inc.,

300 PARK AVENUE SOUTH, NEW YORK, NY 10010

Copyright © **DEBBY BULL**

Book design by **WERNER DESIGN WERKS,** Inc. MINNEAPOLIS

Marty Stuart's vintage costume collection
photographed by **Kyle Ericksen**

The font **HILLBILLY** HOLLYWOOD
was designed especially for this book by Test Pilot Collective

Distributed by St. Martin's Press

PRINTED   AND   BOUND   IN   SINGAPORE

Wardrobe

Dedication

FOR MY MOTHER, REGINA TORGERSON MILLER

This is a book about famous people you've never heard of.

They were the big stars in what is now a ghost town. They were part of a Hollywood that sold tickets to an imaginary West. They wandered to California from real ranches in Texas and Oklahoma, many of them, and they really did know old cowpoke songs and really could ride horses. Then they stepped into a myth.

In the West in the old movies, the good cowboys wore hats that were white, the color of angels, because they kept harm away from the pure places. Blackness couldn't settle over the goodness of the open spaces: the guys in the black hats could never win. The good guys had sweet voices and soft kerchiefs and a posse that backed them up with guitars.

You can tell from their pictures that these cowboys were living in the glow of attention. Along with all the work in the movies, they got record deals and radio shows and played live dances with their bands at places like the Santa Monica Pier. They were all in a big constellation of stars, a corral full of country & Western singers, that was the brightest thing in Los Angeles in the forties.

Looking at these pictures, you see a bunch of white people in fancy, sort of silly-looking clothes. They had never had money before, and they could afford the best clothes, and they wanted to stand out. So they did a hillbilly thing: they got the smart gabardine wool suits with all the fine tailoring, and they put big, bright flowers all over them. **They had the tailors make the clothes actually sparkle: they were stars, after all.** Roy Rogers said his clothes had to have rhinestones so that when the lights hit him as he came into a stadium riding Trigger, even the kids farthest away in the stands could see him.

Hollywood loved these cowboys for a long time, right up until TV came along and delivered Western stories right at home. By the sixties, these cowboys were pretty much gone. You couldn't hear their high voices carrying across the campfire; you heard instead fast drums and guitars driving country songs in a whole new direction. The music was jumping, rocking and rolling. Nobody believed anymore that the world was so simple that a guy in a white hat with a guitar could stop a fight with a song about little doggies.

Singer Johnny Horton

The cowboys who didn't simply quit drifted out of Hollywood. They'd make their records in Nashville, where the big radio show, *The Grand Ole Opry*, would just shut out the noise of rock & roll. They took their wild, embroidered clothes and their sparkling fringe and they left L.A. to the Elvises of the world. **"Rockabilly gave me a nervous breakdown,"** one of these men said.

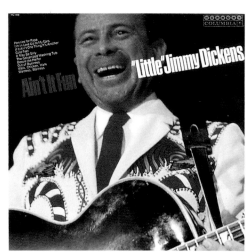

and then t

**left
STY
has la
the p
coun**

To this day, country singers still wear the same clothes, sparkle the same way, have the stitched arrows and Western cut to their jackets, but most of the old cowboys who set the style have been forgotten. There are people in this book who were once the most popular singers in America, but nobody listens to their records anymore and nobody remembers their names. Their lives went from the bottom to the top and back out of sight. The thing you learn from these men, now in their eighties, is that **you make a life out of trying to express yourself, not out of trying to stay popular.** The journeys up and down that they took were long trips in equally interesting directions.

This is a story with an ending like t some good and everyone feels better, can really answer: "Who was that ma **way he looked.**

The cowboys who didn't simply quit drifted out of Hollywood. They'd make their records in Nashville, where the big radio show, *The Grand Ole Opry*, would just shut out the noise of rock & roll. They took their wild, embroidered clothes and their sparkling fringe and they left L.A. to the Elvises of the world. **"Rockabilly gave me a nervous breakdown,"** one of these men said.

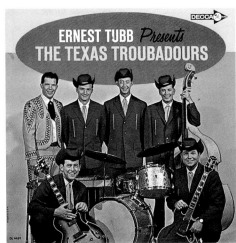
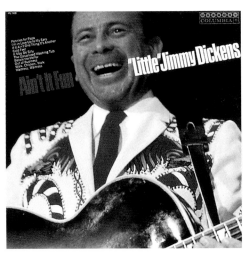

To this day, country singers still wear the same clothes, sparkle the same way, have the stitched arrows and Western cut to their jackets, but most of the old cowboys who set the style have been forgotten. There are people in this book who were once the most popular singers in America, but nobody listens to their records anymore and nobody remembers their names. Their lives went from the bottom to the top and back out of sight. The thing you learn from these men, now in their eighties, is that **you make a life out of trying to express yourself, not out of trying to stay popular.** The journeys up and down that they took were long trips in equally interesting directions.

From this vantage point fifty years down the road, you can see **they have something nobody can take away from them:** they created indelible images of themselves. They invented themselves, made up the whole look and feel and sound of an era, and then they left. **They left behind a STYLE that has lasted up to the present in country music.**

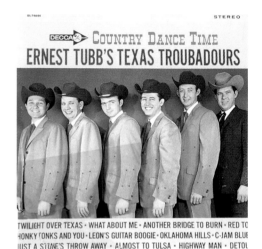

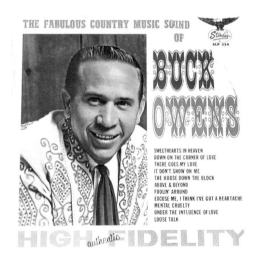

This is a story with an ending like the best Western that was ever on TV, *The Lone Ranger*. In every episode, he rides in, does some good and everyone feels better, and then he disappears from the scene. At the end, everyone asks a question that nobody can really answer: "Who was that masked man?" They don't know his name. **All they can remember is the way he looked.**

EVERY SATUR-

DAY

NIGHT

in 1955, the singing cowboy Tex Ritter hosted a show called *Ranch Party*, which featured Los Angeles country & Western stars singing from the hay bales in a TV barnyard. The regulars included the lanky crooner Wesley Tuttle and his pretty wife Marilyn; a red-headed swing-band vocalist called Carrot Top Anderson; and an Okie sister-and-brother act known as the Collins Kids. Singers who'd made a splash on some radio barn dance in Dallas or Shreveport would stop by to do a song, too, and the show was visited by such fresh-faced newcomers as Carl Perkins, Johnny Cash, George Jones, and Patsy Cline. The show represents the sunniest point in the golden years of country music in Hollywood.

Tex Ritter, right of sign, at a Hollywood premiere

The performers were dressed in fancy Western-tailored suits, flamboyantly embroidered or sparkling in sequins. This was hillbilly Hollywood—equal parts cowboy and show business, Western and honky-tonk, down-home and larger than life. In a tailored cowboy costume covered in big embroidered carrots, Carrot Top Anderson looked both elegant and gaudy, and that was the Hollywood influence that became the essence of country & Western style.

Hillbilly songwriters, pickers, and singers had been drawn to California since the thirties by the promise of work. There were recording contracts with labels like Capitol and 4 Star; there were movie deals at Republic, Monogram, and the other studios churning out B-Westerns; and there were a score of barn-dance radio shows where a new act could get a break.

That's how the Maddox Brothers and Sister Rose made it. A family of migrant fruit pickers led by their dreamer-mother Lula, they'd hitchhiked all the way from Alabama to California during the Depression and clambered out of a radio show in a furniture store to stardom. Lula wanted her kids to wear the fancy clothes that Roy Rogers and Gene Autry wore, so she ordered wildly embroidered Western wear from the same tailor that dressed the singing cowboy stars. **Country & Western style would never recover any decorum after Lula was done.** It's as if Lula herself waved a wand over all the performers on *Ranch Party*.

In the late fifties, though, country & Western had had its heyday in Hollywood. From the stilted opening moments of *Ranch Party* when Marilyn Tuttle waves us all inside the barn to the finale with its lineup of singers dressed like cowboys in a studio corral, the show represents the last gasp of the once all-important country & Western scene in California. The Collins Kids are show stoppers. They seem too fast, though, too rock & roll, for the likes of laid-back Wesley Tuttle and Tex Ritter. You can see in the show the beginning of the end of country & Western in Los Angeles. Rock & roll would take over by the early sixties, and country music would move almost wholly to Nashville.

The L.A. country & Western scene fizzled out so fast that it may seem to be just a prologue to the real history of country music. It was an impressive slice of the country & Western story, though, lasting more than twenty years, grooming some of the biggest stars, and defining the stage-costume style for good. Looking in on *Ranch Party* from a half century away, you can still see in Tex Ritter's corral a look that never was lost.

Lula Maddox, standing by the car; the Maddoxes in Turk finery in the forties; legendary rock producer Phil Spector, in a cowboy hat, with the Ronettes in the sixties as rock & roll took over the recording studios

DRIFTERS, DREAMERS, AND THE FIRST OF THE **Fancy Cowboys**

In 1934, six million people were on public assistance in America; one in every four workers was unemployed. The stock market had crashed in 1929 and nearly half the nation's banks had gone under. The drought in Oklahoma's Dust Bowl from 1934 to 1937 had driven out half the population. Times were so bad that Woody Guthrie said of his mother's singing then, "She commenced to sing the sadder songs in a loster voice."

More than half a million people migrated to the fruit-growing regions of California. Dislocated Southerners, along with the dreamers who were were cutting loose from factories in the industrial cities of the Northeast, were the audience for the mix of plaintive Western ballads and Southern bluegrass and blues that was country music in California. (The music was classified then not as country & Western but as hillbilly/folk.)

For this audience, song lyrics had to pick you up, lift you above a hard, raw life; they were the self-help genre of the time. You can imagine migrants lying in the darkness at night, buoyed by a twanging voice on the radio calling, "Just open up your heart and let the sun shine in."

Stuart Hamblen, a singer and songwriter from Texas, wrote "Let the Sun Shine In" and other upbeat standards, including, "This Old House." In 1928, he was in a string band called the Beverly Hill Billies, who had one of the most popular radio shows in L.A. The loose, backwoods feel of the Hill Billies' show was so convincing that radio listeners actually believed that Appalachian mountain folk who'd wound up in Hollywood came out of the hills for the broadcast. The station brought in a studio audience, and the band dressed the part, in boots and hats. From the start, stage clothes were important in selling country bands.

Stuart **HAMBLEN** gave MANY OF THE COUNTRY & WESTERN STARS OF THE FORTIES THEIR FIRST BREAK, AND HE WAS PROBABLY THE FIRST TO START **FANCY** COUNTRY & WESTERN DRESSING.

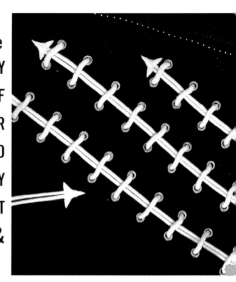

A charismatic storyteller, Hamblen was given more and more radio time until, by 1932, he was on the air every day of the week, doing as many as five hours of live broadcasts a day. He had a show called *The Covered Wagon Jubilee* in the mornings, *The Lucky Stars* in the afternoons, and *King Cowboy and His Western Revue* in the evenings. On Sundays, he even had *The Cowboy Church*. He gave many of the country & Western stars of the forties their first break, and he was probably the first to start fancy country & Western dressing. His signature style was a Western outfit all in black, except for white lacings and pocket trim—an almost elegant cowboy look.

Country & Western Dances in L.A.

Sponsored by the Star Outfitting Company, Hamblen's band the Lucky Stars also played live dances. Country & Western dances took place everywhere from the town hall in Compton to clubs, like the Riverside Rancho and the 97th Street Corral, to outdoor spots like the Santa Monica Pier and Crawford's Market in El Monte. A radio deejay named Bert "Foreman" Phillips promoted country & Western all over L.A. with his Swing Shift dances.

SPADE Cooley, playing at the Santa Monica Pier, was a

popular band leader on Phillips' shows. (His life story's one of the great scandals of pop music: he was tried and convicted for the murder of his wife in 1961, after his career ebbed. Their teenaged daughter, Melody, told the jury she watched as her father dragged her mother, nude, from the shower, kicked her to death and then put a cigarette out on her face.) Cooley was hyped by his record company as the King of Western Swing, but a more worthy candidate for the title was Bob Wills, a Texan who settled in L.A. in 1943. They both outfitted their bands in matching Western wear, more than a dozen players dressed exactly alike down to their boots and bandanas, an outrageous lineup of cookie-cutter cowboys.

Wills, a fiddler himself, added big-band instruments like the piano, saxophone, brasses, and drums to the traditional country guitar and fiddle. His music incorporated Southern blues, Mexican music, and urban swing styles. Western swing music started a dance craze that drew people to the big dance halls in droves.

The steps blended old-fashioned Southern square-dancing with ballroom moves, and the dancers, like the bands, dressed in fancy Western wear. Tex Williams, fronting his band the Western Caravan, even asked a tailor to set up a booth where he was playing so that people could order clothes right at the club.

Broadcast Barn Dances

Sometimes a radio station would capitalize on the popularity of a dance-party venue, like Compton's town hall, and used it as the setting for a radio show, as KFI did for its *Town Hall Party*. (It was this radio broadcast that would later become first a local TV show of the same name and then the syndicated national television show *Ranch Party*.) Radio's barn-dance variety shows, which also included *Hollywood Barn Dance* and Cliffie Stone's *Hometown Jamboree*, introduced a huge audience to country & Western music.

The live-broadcast barn dance was a popular concept even in the twenties; by the forties, it was already being revived. WLS radio's *National Barn Dance* in Chicago started humbly in 1926 with a man who imitated barnyard animals, a square-dance caller, and a Hawaiian guitar duet. By the early thirties, the WLS show featured future country & Western stars **Gene Autry, Lulu Belle and Scotty, and Patsy Montana and the Prairie Ramblers,** who introduced their hit, "I Want to Be a Cowboy's Sweetheart" on the show in 1935.

By the forties, shows around the country, like *The Big D Jamboree* in Dallas and Shreveport's *Louisiana Hayride*, served as a springboard to the popular *Grand Ole Opry* in Nashville and television and movie appearances in Hollywood. Even Cincinnati had a barn dance, *The Boone County Jamboree*, which was broadcast at 500,000 watts and literally heard around the world. Singer Wesley Tuttle headed to Cincinnati in 1940 for a stint on *The Boone County Jamboree*; the show was so popular that when Tuttle headed back to California and recorded his first record, "I Dreamed that My Daddy Came Home," it immediately sold over 100,000 copies.

The Cowboys' Tailor, **Nathan Turk**

Like almost all of the country & Western singers on the radio, Wesley Tuttle had his first stage clothes made by Nathan Turk, who opened a cleaning and tailoring shop in North Hollywood in 1928. The shop was just down the street from Republic Studios, so cowboy stars and would-be cowboys stopped in to ask Turk, a Polish immigrant who loved Western movies, to design and sew a suit of clothes.

Nathan Turk made fine-tailored suits in expensive gabardines, using Western design elements like the arrowhead at the ends of the "smile" pockets (with no pocket flap). He also made shirts with leather lacings at the neck instead of buttons. He dressed all of the movie cowboys, and it was Roy Rogers who gave Lula Maddox his name. Turk's outfits for the Maddox Brothers and Rose earned them the billing "the Most Colorful Hillbilly Band in America."

Lula Maddox took the family to California in 1933, hauling her six kids aged seven to sixteen. For years, they followed the crops from the San Joaquin Valley to the Imperial Valley in a 1931 Ford. When they became a popular radio act in the forties, after all those depressing years, Lula was not about to order a somber set of outfits for her kids.

The outfits Turk made for the Maddoxes were the first of their kind: embroidered, flashy, brightly colored and, because they were so beautifully tailored, a little elegant, as well. The boys asked for bell bottoms instead of straight-legged cowboy pants; they liked the look of sailors' pants. And they wanted short jackets like Eisenhower wore. The shirts, worn under suit jackets that were often taken off because of the heat, were bright satins covered in chain-stitched flowers. By 1944, each band member had his own Fleetwood Cadillac and twenty-five complete outfits of clothes. And Turk had lots of customers asking for the same sort of flamboyant stage clothes. They were a performer's spin on cowboy clothes, an extension of flashy rodeo style. It was a perfect look for movie cowboys who spent more time in parades and public appearances than before the cameras.

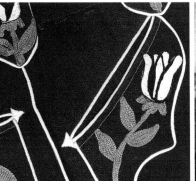  

These costumes exaggerated the styles of the original Western stars Tom Mix, Buck Jones, Ken Maynard, and Hoot Gibson. Jones was even quoted as complaining, as his star was eclipsed by the singing cowboys', that kids got "the wrong idea that all you need to stop an Indian or a rustler is a loud voice accompanied by a hillbilly band."

TURK'S OUTFITS FOR THE MADDOX BROTHERS AND ROSE EARNED THEM THE BILLING "the Most Colorful Hillbilly Band in America"

The Movie COWBOYS

From about 1914 on, the movie studios churned out Westerns that starred cowboy heroes like those in the dime novels and real-life adventure magazines that were popular at the time. In the mid-thirties, what came to be called the horse opera, the Western with a singing-cowboy star, created a whole new interest in cowboy movies. In 1934, Gene Autry was asked, simply on the strength of his record sales, to costar in a movie with Ken Maynard. Soon Autry's evocative, lonely voice was carrying across the movie plains. After he'd settled in L.A., Autry asked Nathan Turk to copy the brightly colored, embroidered rodeo clothes he'd brought west from Chicago. Autry and Champion, his horse, went on to make over ninety Western movies. Autry also hosted a radio show called *The Melody Ranch* from 1939 to 1956.

By 1938, another actor in the Westerns was competing with Autry at the box office. Leonard Slye had moved to L.A. from Ohio, hoping to make it as a country & Western singer. He first changed his name to Dick Westin and formed one of the most important early country & Western music acts, the Sons of the Pioneers. The Sons of the Pioneers also had their own radio show, featuring their plaintive harmony-singing, clip-clop rhythms, and lyrics that romanticized the landscape of the West. As he moved on to the movies, the singer was asked to change his name again: **he picked Roy** (vetoing the studio's choice, **Leroy) and Rogers** (for Will). In 1944, Roy Rogers was cast opposite a blonde comedic actress named Dale Evans in a movie called *The Cowboy and the Señorita*. The two married in 1947. They were the subject of a million photos but **refused to kiss for the cameras because, Roy said, "The kids wouldn't like it."**

Both Autry and Rogers had solid music talent that they brought to the movies: they were both songwriters and singers who had previously had success on the radio. Many of the movies' other singing cowboys also had Western dance bands, and country & Western singers often appeared in films: it was the original cross-plugging. Roy Acuff, after making "Wabash Cannonball" a gold record, appeared in *My Darling Clementine*, *Cowboy Canteen*, and *Night Train to Memphis*. Even Ernest Tubb, while cutting million-sellers like "Walking the Floor over You," was filming B-Westerns like *Fightin' Buckaroos* and *Ridin' West*.

Tex
Ritter, however, probably best straddled the worlds of music and movies. At the University of Texas in Austin, he befriended John Lomax, a serious collector of cowboy songs, who published *Cowboy Songs and Other Frontier Ballads* in 1910. Ritter dropped out of law school and traveled to New York, where he hosted a radio show called *Tex Ritter's Campfire*, which helped make cowboy songs vogue in the early thirties. He moved to Hollywood in 1936 and starred in over seventy Westerns. As the first big country & Western artist signed to the fledgling Capitol label in 1942, he also had a string of hit records, including "Hillbilly Heaven."

Chain-stitching on Turk costumes; Henry Maddox, who played mandolin; Turk costume detail; Gene Autry (right)

Country & Western Recording Stars

The roster of artists at Capitol was unmatched and produced many of the biggest hit records of the postwar years. It included Ritter, Tuttle, Tex Williams, Jimmy Wakely, Merle Haggard, Faron Young, Freddie Hart, Jean Shepard, Joe Maphis, Wynn Stewart, Buck Owens, Merle Travis, Wanda Jackson, and the Louvin Brothers. The company had just begun to press vinyl records again, after a hiatus during the war years. They published their own fan magazine, *The Capitol Record News*, and advertised in magazines like *Tophand*, which focused exclusively on the California country & Western scene.

Wesley Tuttle actually went to audition at Capitol with his buddy Merle Travis, whose style, a hybrid of folk and honky-tonk, still influences country & Western guitarists. It was Tuttle who was signed first, though, not Travis; the A&R man thought that the name "Wesley Tuttle" had a more commercial ring to it. Travis, working as a bit player in the movies, honed his songwriting skill and eventually landed a string of chart hits for Capitol, including "Divorce Me C.O.D.," "So Round, So Firm, So Fully Packed," and "Sixteen Tons."

In 1946, Hank Thompson was discharged from the navy and also headed west for a career with Capitol, after Tex Ritter heard the singer-guitarist and his Western swing band, the Brazos Valley Boys, and recommended them to his label. Thompson's "Humpty Dumpty Heart" and "Today" were huge hits in 1948, and "The Wild Side of Life" was a million-seller in 1952 (and answered by the Kitty Wells hit, "It Wasn't God Who Made Honky Tonk Angels").

Another country & Western hit-maker based in L.A. at the time was Lefty Frizzell, who'd perfected his honky-tonk style, with his laid-back vocals, in Waco, Texas. Signed with Columbia Records, Frizzell scored a huge chart hit in 1950 with "If You've Got the Money, I've Got the Time," and followed that with two Number One records in "I Want to Be with You Always" and "Always Late." Columbia had Johnny Horton and Jimmy Dickens, too, whose early records hint at the rockabilly movement to come.

MAYBE THE BEST-SELLING WESTERN SWING RECORD OF ALL TIME, **TEX WILLIAMS'** "SMOKE, SMOKE, SMOKE (THAT CIGARETTE)," COWRITTEN WITH MERLE TRAVIS, SOLD NEARLY TWO AND A HALF MILLION RECORDS FOR CAPITOL, TURNING WILLIAMS INTO AN INTERNATIONAL STAR.

Williams sold a horse to give money to help a young tailor named Nudie Cohen start a business in the back of a club called the Palace Barn. Nudie took his cues from Turk's successful Western-wear business but pushed the outlandish decoration to the limits.

NUDIE COHEN: Flash and Sparkle

By 1949, Nudie established the infamous Nudie's Rodeo Tailors in North Hollywood and would go on to outfit nearly every country & Western singer and singing cowboy in Los Angeles. When Roy Rogers worried that people in the far seats at his arena shows couldn't see him, he asked Nudie to add rhinestones to his fancy cowboy clothes. Nudie soon had nearly every country & Western singer sparkling. Lefty Frizzell got one of the first shirts Nudie made that had rhinestones on the fringe.

The tailor also became known for making suits that played off themes from the singers' records or their names. Hank Thompson ordered a suit that Nudie covered with hearts that tumbled down the sleeves and pants, for a hit record called "Humpty Dumpty Heart." Webb Pierce got shirts covered in spider's webs; Ferlin Husky got husky dogs on his jackets.

Porter Wagoner had NUDIE make up a rainbow of colored suits for himself and all the WAGON MASTERS all of them featuring wagon wheels.

By the time the L.A. country & Western acts were introduced on television to the rest of the country, they were likely to be dressed by Nudie. Though the shop stayed in North Hollywood, Nudie and his wife Bobbie soon found they had to travel to Nashville to meet their country-music customers.

A rainbow of Nudie jackets for Porter Wagoner's band

Country & Western Shifts to Nashville

By 1960, little was left of the Los Angeles country & Western scene. Cowboys had practically been more at home in Hollywood than out on the range, and now all the hayseed seemed hokey. Even the seminal country & Western TV show, *Town Hall Party*, the local Los Angeles broadcast that developed into the syndicated *Ranch Party*, had been deserted by Tex Ritter and Wesley Tuttle and was featuring guest stars like future rock icons Gene Vincent and Eddie Cochran and their rockabilly bands.

Capitol sought the rockabilly and rock & roll hit makers, leaving RCA and other labels in Nashville to scoop up the country market. Nashville's Saturday-night radio show, *The Grand Ole Opry*, continued to thrive, but the music, having left the simpler Western elements behind, was now just called country. After the early sixties, "hillbilly" was considered a derogatory description. The singers who sparkled, like Porter Wagoner and Conway Twitty, were smoother pop stylists than their L.A. counterparts had been.

This pop country strain, appealing to a more sentimental audience, held sway until the seventies. Though **Buck Owens** and **Merle Haggard** continued throughout the sixties to create a more raucous, honky-tonk kind of music, their isolation in Bakersfield, California, kept Nashville from even recognizing them. By 1973, Waylon Jennings, aligning himself with **Willie Nelson, Johnny Cash,** and outlaws in general, defined a rebellious new strain of country music right in Nashville.

These singers brought a rougher, more Western sensibility to country music; Jennings even charted in 1974 with a song called "Bob Wills Is Still the King." To distance themselves further from what appeared to be tired country trappings, the outlaws rejected the old Nudie clothes. The two strains of country—one more pop and the other more rock, the first in rhinestones and the second in jeans—were at odds.

At the same time, out in L.A., **GRAM PARSONS** and his influential country-rock band, the **Flying Burrito Brothers,** decked themselves out in Nudie clothes. Fusing elements of the pure country music that he must've heard on the radio in Florida when he was a kid, like the lovely harmonies of the Louvin Brothers, with rock & roll, Gram Parsons, first with the Byrds and later with the Burritos, helped create a synthesis of music styles that had seemed at cross-purposes. Those bands pulled the best of country, the plaintiveness of the lyrics and simplicity of the music, to the stripped-down delivery of a rock band. They made country cool with a rock audience, while exposing it for the first time to the over-the-top clothes of Nudie's Rodeo Tailors.

They made country COOL with a rock audience, while exposing it for the first time to the OVER-THE-TOP CLOTHES of Nudie's Rodeo Tailors.

Merle Haggard at the Opry

GRAM PARSONS (upper right) **AND THE FLYING BURRITO BROTHERS**

The HILLBILLY COMEBACK and the Clothes of MANUEL

Not until the early eighties did the gap between the three strains of country music begin to close, with a burgeoning country-roots music scene in L.A. that took much of its inspiration from the danceable, raw country & Western music that had grown up there and a little from country-rock as well. In 1986, Dwight Yoakam released an album called *Guitars, Cadillacs, etc., etc.*–a song line that actually ended, "…and hillbilly music." Embraced by the rock world, the ground-breaking album featured covers of songs by Johnny Horton and Harlan Howard, both part of the L.A.-based country & Western scene of the forties, and was recorded at Capitol's Hollywood studios.

Yoakam brazenly connected himself to the rough-edged country & Western sound

that country had tried to "mature" away from. The next year, he released an album entitled *Hillbilly Deluxe*, which featured a cover version of Lefty Frizzell's 1951 hit, "Always Late," another homage to the California country & Western scene. Even Yoakam's clothes were a nod to that era: he was outfitted by Manuel Cuevas, who had apprenticed at Nudie's shop and was at one time his son-in-law.

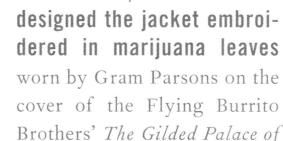

At Nudie's, **MANUEL** designed the jacket embroidered in marijuana leaves worn by Gram Parsons on the cover of the Flying Burrito Brothers' *The Gilded Palace of Sin*. In the seventies, he opened his own tailoring shop in North Hollywood. Another country artist who came to Manuel for stage clothes was **Marty Stuart,** a guitarist who'd left home at thirteen to pick with Lester Flatt and later toured for nine years with Johnny Cash. Stuart called his own 1989 solo record *Hillbilly Rock* and dressed his band in vintage costumes, which he collected.

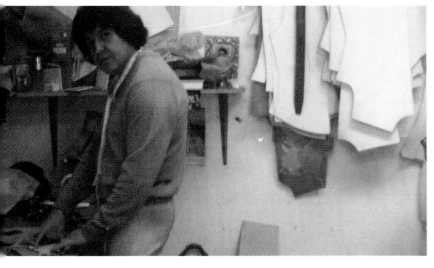

In 1987, Manuel also made the clothes for **Emmylou Harris, Dolly Parton,** and **Linda Ronstadt** for the cover of their first *Trio* album. Their embrace of the tradition of Nudie-style costumes, along with that of Yoakam and Stuart, helped bring back the old style of dress. Today there is hardly a popular country & Western performer, including **Tricia Yearwood, Randy Travis,** and **Wynonna,** who is not outfitted by Manuel, now based in Nashville, or occasionally wearing vintage Nudie or Turk.

Manuel at the cutting table in his North Hollywood shop

Lyle Lovett, who tours with a big country & Western band, has said, **"Bill Monroe and his Bluegrass Boys always wore suits. So we always wear suits."** And it's not just country performers who have returned to these roots. Beck wears vintage Western shirts, and Sheryl Crow often dons a cowboy hat, and both rock singers contributed songs to a CD tribute to Gram Parsons, rock's ultimate Nudie fan. Even Brandy and rap stars like Will Smith, fresh from the full cowboy regalia of *Wild Wild West*, Salt-N-Pepa and Lil' Kim took to wearing cowboy hats in their videos.

All of this interest in cowboy style and in swing dancing, spurred by the infamous "Khakis Swing" Gap ad, has sent collectors hunting for the vintage Western wear once worn by club goers of the forties. Along with Nudie and Turk clothes, labels from the shops of Rodeo Ben, in Philadelphia (the owner of the restaurant 21 bought $15,000 of Ben Cantor's cowboy clothes in the forties), Viola Grae or Minnie Fox, out of Hollywood, and Fay Ward, in New York, are among the most collectible.

Western style that is at once very fine and almost goofy is also getting reinvented today as high fashion: Gucci's embroidered and beaded wool pants were the haute couture hit of 1999 and every bit as off-the-wall as Nudie's work. Cowboy hats, cowboy boots, and fringed leather were featured in shows the same year by Tommy Hilfiger, Valentino, Anna Sui, and Givenchy.

The names of Lula Maddox and Nathan Turk, two people who dreamed of groves of orange trees and movie cowboys and made their way to California, are not well known. The way they outfitted the young Rose Maddox and her brothers, however—a riot of roses bursting over bright gabardines—has been unforgettable: one inspired idea that caught the light and never stopped sparkling. "The SOUND SYSTEMS were so lousy back then that the crowd couldn't hear the music," Buck Owens, who used to duet with Rose, recalled, summing it all up, "so the clothes had to be loud."

Marty Stuart in a jacket by Manuel; Dwight Yoakam

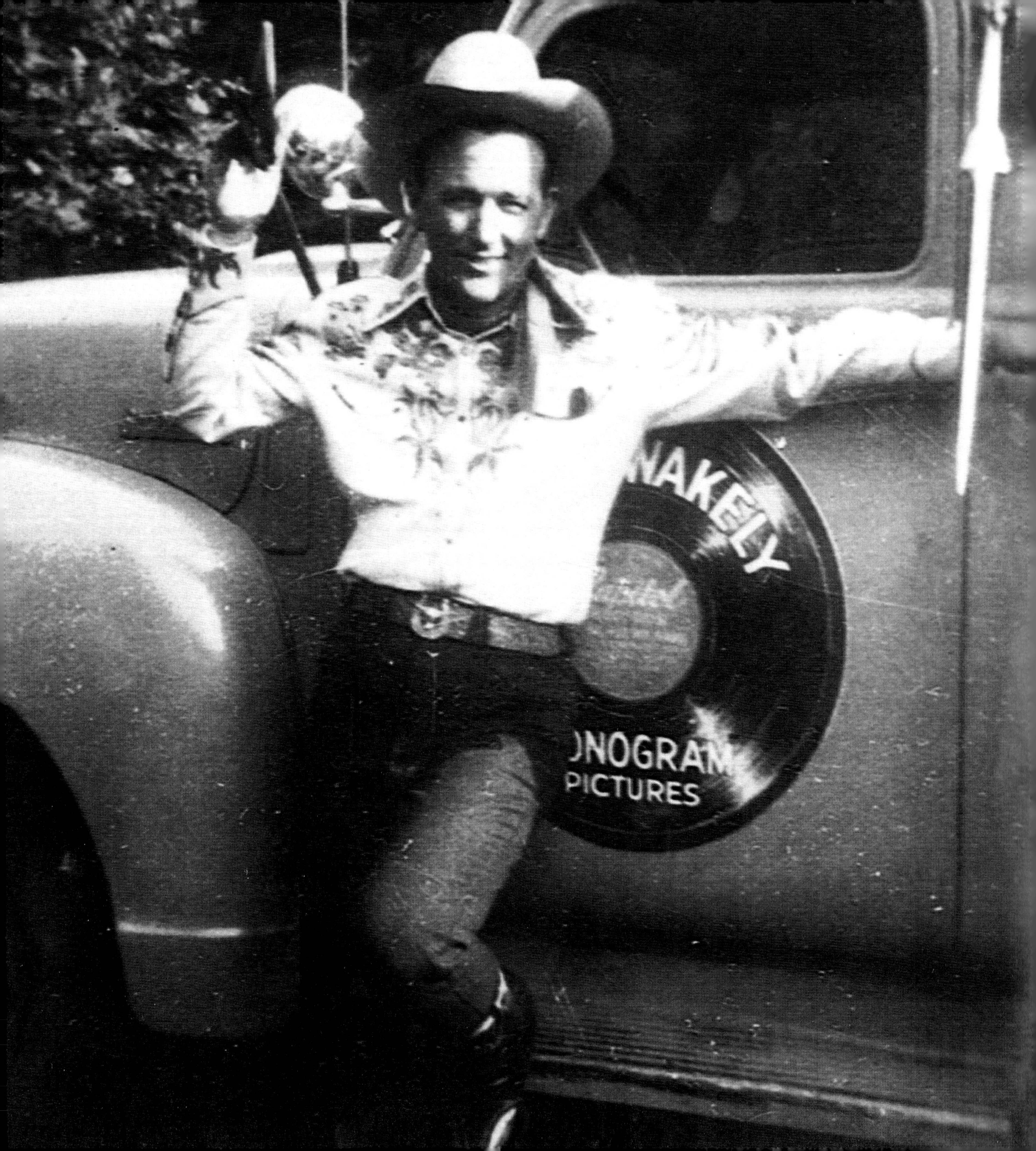
NAKELY
ONOGRAM
PICTURES

May God Bless You

Ferlin Husky

GENE AUTRY

(Western-movie icon): **I was a very lucky young man—Tom Mix couldn't sing,** so I was the first of the singing cowboys. They called me a yodeling cowboy back in those days. The guy who had the rodeo in Chicago made all the cowboys wear a flashy shirt—red or silver. He said, "I want the cowboys to look like the ones they read about in the Wild West magazines."

Jean Turk Simon *(daughter of tailor Nathan Turk):* When the Republic Studios were just starting in Studio City, and that was a real cowboy scene, with real horses. The cowboys would come in and chat and look for clothes, and they'd ask my dad if he could fix them up something. He just developed a style for them over a period of many years. I remember he was always fascinated by cowboy and Indian movies, that part of Hollywood. He went to all those early movies. And he'd get books and look intently at the pictures, how the people were dressed, and it grew from there.

Manuel Cuevas *(tailor):* The cowboys had a rough sense of copying the Native Americans. They wore overshirts and dresses like Daniel Boone and Davy Crockett wore. They traded with the Indians and bought big dresses and wore them as shirts. The arrowhead design came from the Indians. The Aztec and American Indians all have arrows in their designs. The Spanish conquistadors adapted it. **They were the only ones who came to America with a sense of dressage.**

Eddie Dean *(singing cowboy who wrote the classic country song, "I Dreamed of a Hillbilly Heaven"):* Western music was a pictorial-type music; country was more of the love part of it. The cowboys did sing love songs, but it was more of a tongue-in-cheek kind of thing, like this song I did in one of my pictures–"You're as pretty as a palomino pony"–singing that to a girl. "You're a gal for whom a guy could write a song, but the cattle must be tended, so I must be moseying along." It's a different type of love song. Most of those Western songs were done in pictures more than on records. Gene Autry had "Back in the Saddle," but that was in the pictures–that was a basic Western song. Autry's "That Silver-Haired Daddy of Mine" was more of a country-type song.

Roy Rogers *(singing cowboy in movies and the ultimate Western TV star):* **Country was music from Kentucky or Tennessee, and Western music was from Texas.** The tempo was different, but the songs were the same. I made my first picture in 1938. They had a lot of country singers in L.A., and the they'd make personal appearances in my pictures. Like we'd bring out Jimmy Wakely from Oklahoma, and he'd make an appearance in my picture. That way we'd get publicity both ways.

Les "Carrot Top" Anderson *(singer in early Wester-swing bands and TV performer):* I joined Bob Wills' band, playing steel guitar, in Tulsa in 1942, and then we went to California. Bob Wills deserves all the credit he got for inventing Western swing, and then some. When I left Bob Wills, I went with Spade Cooley in 1947 as the featured vocalist. With Spade, the band all dressed alike. The uniforms were black, trimmed in white, with a big black spade trimmed in white on the front. We played dances at the Santa Monica Pier. There were all kinds of guests, even an elephant.

Hank Thompson *(singer and band leader):* I grew up with the real country music of Jimmie Rodgers, the Carter Family, Vernon Dalhart—the early country recording artists—and Gene Autry, Roy Acuff, Ernest Tubb, and *The Grand Ole Opry* on the radio. Of course, down South, we had the Light Crust Doughboys, Milton Brown. I grew up listening to all of it. I went through boot camp for the navy in San Diego. There was a lot of country music out there at that time. The first time I saw Ernest Tubb was at the Venice Pier while I was in the service. So many of the people from Texas and Oklahoma migrated to California during the war years. There was work out there at the war plants and the shipyards. That culture moved with them and led to the popularity of Southwestern music on the West Coast.

Jean Shepard *(singer):* I moved to California with my parents about six months before World War II ended. I was only eleven or twelve. It was a matter of survival. The Depression had taken its toll on so many farmers. My father became a foreman on a ranch in California. We picked cotton and picked peaches and oranges, cut grapes, to make a living. In the peach orchards, people would give me a bushel of peaches if I'd sing a song. We had listened to *The Grand Ole Opry* for years on an old battery radio in Oklahoma. We were very well-acquainted with country music. There were no women singers on the *Opry*, though, so I didn't have much to pick from for musical influences. I just would hear a song and sing it. There were no women singers to go back to. I got started when I got together with this group of girls from school—one played piano, one played guitar, and I sang. We called ourselves the Melody Ranch Girls. Back then, we wore matching Western pants and shirts, with cowboy boots.

Gene Autry: When I started making pictures, I got the idea to dress in loud, colorful cowboy clothes from the early days of Tom Mix. He was an old-line cowboy, except he wore a very nice cowboy Western look. My clothes were all cut with a Western look. I never wore glitter but I had riders who entered when we made appearances, all of them in a different-colored shirt in iridescent fabric.

Suzy Hamblen *(wife of radio star Stuart Hamblen):* All of the country & Western acts would appear live at the movie houses, playing with their bands between the two shows of a double feature. Personal appearances were a big deal back when there was no television. Stuart was the first of the country & Western singers to start wearing tailor-made cowboy outfits, in the twenties. He started about the same time as the early Western-movie stars, like Ken Maynard. Stuart wore tailored Western outfits. He never went for the rhinestones. Mostly, he wore outfits in black, with white lacings and pipings, with the tailored pocket detail. He had roses embroidered on his shirts and wore white chaps. They were smart-looking, not flashy. Stuart worked in some pictures, several with Roy Rogers. **He was always the bad guy and got killed every possible way.**

Eddie Dean: I started wearing fancy cowboy clothes because it was sort of a necessity for a leading man to do. **I thought it was a gimmick.** Of course, I was raised in Levi's.

Gene Autry: **When I went in the service,** Roy had to wear my clothes, **because they matched the footage the studio already had.** There was a lot of my background footage. IN ROY'S FIRST PICTURE, HE'S MORE SUBDUED AS A DRESSER, LIKE ME. LATER, ROY'S CLOTHES HAD MORE PIZZAZZ. Republic didn't want a cookie-cutter effect. They wanted the two of us to have different looks. I think Republic tried to make it seem like Roy and I were enemies.

Roy Rogers: I started that fancy cowboy dressing, and Gene probably didn't want to follow me, because I did it.

We were always competitors.

Roy (left) and Gene in The Old Corral. *Rogers was cast opposite Autry, who, in a movie fight scene, forced him to sing at gunpoint.*

Rose Maddox *(lead singer, the Maddox Brothers and Sister Rose):* We started wearing fancy stage clothes in 1948, after the boys came back from the service. Nathan Turk made all of our clothes. **It was my mother's idea to dress us up like that.** She was the boss of the band, the head of the herd. We gave him an idea, and he took it from there. It was something people had never seen before, a whole group dressed alike in those wild clothes.

Irwin Simon *(son-in-law of tailor Nathan Turk):* Rose Maddox was special, she and her brothers. **The idea to make their clothes so wild was Nathan's.** We had people that did the embroidery. He'd say, "I'd like this and this on the front, this on the sleeves." He'd design it.

Lacings—that was one of Mr. Turk's designs, the lacing across the yoke, both front and back. The ideas came out of his head. He was extremely creative. He'd dream up these styles. He'd do any color. He'd come up with things, like, "How about making this chartreuse for Rose?" We'd use a basic color, and then put the embroidery on to be really showy.

Roy Rogers, Gene Autry, they all came in for fittings. We did a lot of stuff for Republic Pictures. We kept cardboard patterns for the size of Roy Rogers or Gene Autry, for shirts, coats, and pants.

Rose Maddox: I wore what I thought a woman's Western outfit should look like. Dale Evans wore something like that. I had two- and three-piece outfits, with the skirt, the satin blouse to match it, and the bolero jacket to go over it. And they matched my brothers' outfits. One whole outfit would cost $400 to $600. We had the shirts made to look like the pants, so that we still had a complete outfit if we wanted to take the jackets off, like in the summer when it was too hot to wear the jackets. And I always wore cowboy boots. I would have those made at Lucchese's in San Antonio. I usually used white boots trimmed with silver, so they'd match any of the outfits. And white cowboy hats. **I was a trendsetter. They all tried to copy me.**

Hank Thompson: When I first came out to California, Turk was the only one making Western suits. He made them for Gene Autry, Roy Rogers, Ernest Tubb, Pee Wee King—they wore the fancy suits first. I got a couple of Turk suits. They cost $125 back then. Expensive!

From the old Ford to the new Cadillacs: the Maddox Brothers and Rose hit the road.

Marty Stuart *(country & Western performer and collector of vintage costumes):* Of the old clothes I found, the more tasteful suits, the prettier suits, had a whole different style to them. I'd look at the label, and they all said *N. Turk*. I thought Turk had a really tasteful slant on things, and he dressed the Maddox Brothers and Rose.

They were working the circuit during the most difficult time of our country's history, the Depression. To see this wildcat hillbilly band that played wonderful music come rolling into a Dust Bowl town or a starving orange-grove town in this caravan of identical Cadillacs must have been a sight to behold. You know something's going to happen if these people actually get their guitars around their necks. The lesson of the Maddox Brothers and Rose is that after people came and paid their hard-earned money to see the show, they didn't lose the problems they came in with, but they went out with a smile on their faces and something to talk about for the next few days. It gave them a little more energy to deal with their problems.

This is my favorite story about Rose Maddox: They were Alabama people. Rose's mom, Lula, read a book about California that talked about the oranges on the trees, the gold. She was hit in the heart by all that. She loaded up all her boys, and they went across the country on a freight train. They were so poor, and they had it so tough, that **one time her mama actually tried to give Rose away.**

Rose Lee Maphis *(singer and wife of guitarist Joe Maphis):* We thought of the Maddox Brothers and Rose as the best-dressed people in country & Western. There were five of them up there, all dressed alike! It was very effective. The first time I really bought fancy Western clothes, my girlfriend Mary and I were in a duet called the Saddle Sweethearts. There was a tailor in Philadelphia named Rodeo Ben, and we got a couple of costumes made by him in 1949. They were a cream gabardine with green appliquéd figures, scrolling.

Irwin Simon: Turk came to the U.S. in 1911, when he was seventeen. Conditions were too bad in Poland. He came to America alone. He came in at Ellis Island. He met Bessie, Mrs. Turk, in New York. They both worked in sweatshops. He didn't like New York. They moved to California, to the Valley, bought property, and built a little house. That area was remote at the time. Turk started with a little cleaning establishment in the front, then he started with repairs, and **he did such nice work,** people asked him to make other things. They opened the shop in 1928 or 1929. Turk kept making clothes and gave up cleaning. The Turks had two daughters–Jean and Pearl. I married Jean. I worked in the shop for thirty-five years. I remember that we used to have a lot of pictures in the window, and there was one of Roy Rogers. The inscription read, "Thank you for the clothes on my first picture."

Jean Turk Simon: I was a year old when my parents moved to L.A. in 1920. Nathan wasn't going to L.A. to be a tailor. He wanted to go West, where the weather was good and the orange trees grew. I don't think the movies brought him out here; I think it was just because it was supposed to be very beautiful. They wanted to get out of the crowded ghetto. After they started the business in California, there were some great years. It's a feeling I've always had **that my dad was very well-liked.** He had a lot of charisma. I think the young actors and singers just liked to come to the shop.

Doye O'Dell *(TV cowboy):* Turk's was just a small tailor's shop. He made dress cowboy suits. The country singers wore the same thing as the singing cowboys. From the boots to the hats, there wasn't much difference. On TV, I just wore pants and a tailor-made shirt. **No fringe though, I didn't go for that.**

Gene Autry: Turk was a Jewish man from New York, and he didn't have any idea at first what a cowboy's shirts should look like. I showed him the shirts I'd had made in Chicago. Later on, Nudie started copying my clothes. He brightened them up and made them really, really loud. **He really got carried away.**

Carrot Top Anderson: Cowboy singers were cowboys, and Western singers, like myself, were Western swing, dance music. There was quite a difference in the music, but we all wore the same Western clothes.

Hank Thompson: All the Western swing bands were good. I particularly liked Spade Cooley's. I thought his music was more polished than Bob Wills'. And then later, I liked Tex Williams' band. I liked the West Coast sound. I tailored my own music to be in between Bob Wills, Spade Cooley, that type, and the country type, like Ernest Tubb. The Western swing bands, the vocalist was not the thing; the vocalist was part of the arrangement, the same way it was in the big-band era. The singers were incidental. For Bob Wills, Tommy Duncan was the vocalist; Spade Cooley had Tex Williams and later Carrot Top Anderson. With me, I came out to be the featured vocalist but had a Western swing band with me. **I tailored the music for the band to back me,** not me be a part of the band—it was Hank Thompson and the Brazos Valley Boys.

Carrot Top Anderson: After I started to be called Carrot Top, I went home and stayed up all night, trying to draw a pattern or something out of the nickname. **I finally came up with the little carrot man.** And I went out to Turk's and showed it to him. He said, "Oh, that's great!" He made me up a suit. It was black and pink, of all things. Oh, it was gaudy! I said, "I can't wear that." He said, "Take it and wear it."

I wore the thing once on *Leo Carillo's Dude Ranch Varieties.* I didn't let anybody say anything about the suit, and I didn't say anything about it. **And I got two mailbags full of mail about it. Everybody thought it was WONDERFUL.** In 1952 and 1953, I was the number one male Western vocalist in the country.

BUCK OWENS:
Turk made lots of my costumes. I never knew much about Turk, because I never saw him anywhere outside of his tailor shop. Turk and his family did most of their stuff in a little bitty place. In Turk's shop, he had four or five people in the back. He supervised it all. His wife worked there, and there were seamstresses or guys cutting or sewing in the back. It had a couple of little rooms, where you could have a fitting. **TURK WAS QUICK.** They'd work all day and all night for you to get it on time.

Jean Turk Simon: Nathan was the baby of the family. In Poland, he'd apprenticed to a tailor at ten or eleven years old. The people in the villages, when their kids were that age, looked for a good trade for their young people. Dad went to a tailor. He lived in the people's house and worked and learned, and that's where he picked up the beginning of the trade. The older sisters sent for him after they went to New York. A lot of the things, he trained himself. As he got older, he learned about different fabrics and designs. **He had a real flair for design.** That he developed by himself.

Jean Shepard: I had a couple of Turk uniforms—one was turquoise with gold fringe and the other was a tomato red with lots of flowers and rhinestones. And they were like culottes, a split skirt. That was 1952 or 1953. Back then, the legal age to do anything was twenty-one, and when Ferlin Husky and I went on the road, they had to sign Ferlin as my legal guardian to take me across the state line.

Rose Maddox: We traveled on the road in four or five matching Cadillacs. There was no such thing as tour buses back then. We never ironed the clothes out on the road. There was a rod that we hung across the back of the car, and we kept the clothes on hangers in the car. We would take about six outfits along, enough to last for the length of the tour. We never got them cleaned out on the road. We only used a cleaner in Hollywood. He did them all by hand. We'd always wait until we got back home to take the clothes in to be done there, and then we'd pick up a different set and go back out on the road. We probably had about a dozen outfits, always matching. People were just in awe of our clothes. They'd never seen anything like that. It was half of our show.

Dottie Ethridge *(sister of country & Western singer Charline Arthur):* Charline worked with Rose Maddox some. I think that's where Charline got a lot of her ideas about how the first thing they notice is what you're dressed in.

First you get their ATTENTION by the way you're dressed. And then second, you have to leave them wanting more.

Carrot Top Anderson: Turk probably made twenty of the carrot suits, all in different colors. There was a white one and a black one, and maroon and blue—I had every color. The outfits Turk made were something that people would remember when they didn't remember anything else. If I hadn't had talent, though, that suit wouldn't have meant anything.

Dottie Ethridge: Charline wanted to sing like Ernest Tubb. Her and Sonny James and Hank Locklin were the stars of *The Big D Jamboree*. That was how she met Patsy Cline. She taught Patsy a lot–breathing, bandstand presence, and diction. **PATSY had a lot of potential, and CHARLINE taught her how to use it.** Charline had learned so much working in a medicine show. Patsy and Charline became quite close.

Charline also worked a lot with Elvis Presley. Charline toured with him a long time before he became "the King," so to speak. I don't care if you've heard stories and stories, everybody claiming to have discovered Elvis Presley…Colonel Tom Parker got after Charline, and he started to tell her the rules of his contract. He said, "You will sleep when I tell you to sleep and eat when I tell you to eat." Charline was a real rebel. She said, "Wait a minute, Parker. There ain't no m.f. gonna take fifty per cent of my salary and rule my life. Uh-uh. There ain't gonna be no days like that for Charline Arthur." She said, "I'll tell you what. There's a little guy working in this club down here, not too far, go watch him. He sings like a Negro, but he's a white boy. He's terrific. He's got all the potential." So he went and saw Elvis and signed him. He took and made a slave out of Elvis.

Irwin Simon: Hank Williams, Sr.–Mr. Turk made some things for him. Hank and Audrey opened a shop in Nashville, and we made the clothes for them. All the business was pretty much word-of-mouth. We made clothes for them all. Dale Evans liked the way Nathan would create things for her. Out of the blue, he'd dream things up for her, using embroidery to make desert scenes or cacti or roses. **He'd create the designs off the top of his head, that was his genius. He could draw. He was creative.** Mr. Turk wore a Western shirt and Western pants. He spoke with a little accent.

When Nudie opened, there were not good feelings there. Nudie would come and look in the window of the shop, then he'd take full credit for having created a design. We closed the shop in 1981, because Nathan was ill. We sold all the pictures that had been in the window, and we gave the old patterns away. He died in 1988 at ninety-four. He and Bessie had been married seventy years.

Roy Rogers: We never got really fancy until Nudie came out. Nudie came out here and didn't have any money, so I let him have some money to help him get started. He paid me back, which is unusual in Hollywood. He started making fancy clothes. I'd be playing in places like Madison Square Garden, and I'd be introduced and come in, and I'd be way away from the people. Nudie made me a suit with some rhinestones on it, and I'd come through there and the spotlights would hit me, and I just lit up the whole place. I got him to put more and more rhinestones on the clothes. I'd light up the whole arena.

Rose Lee Maphis: We didn't live too far from Nudie, so we got all our costumes from Nudie's. Once he made us coral suits. Joe couldn't have the rhinestones. When Joe was playing the guitar, he'd twist it around and put it on his back, then pick up and play the banjo. Then the banjo would be hanging there in front, and he'd pick up and play the fiddle. He would constantly be scratching the instruments with the rhinestones.

"Nudie made me a suit with some rhinestones on it, and I'd come through there and the **SPOTLIGHTS would hit me, and I just lit up the whole place.** I got him to put more and more rhinestones on the clothes." *–Roy Rogers*

Buck Owens: "When I worked with Rose Maddox, it was hard to see us for the sparkles."

Bobbie Cohen *(wife of Nudie Cohen and shopkeeper at Nudie's Rodeo Tailors):* Nudie started tailoring in Russia when he was eleven years old. He was apprenticed to a tailor at that early age. After he came here, he worked in sewing factories all over New York City. His brother owned a brassiere company. In 1936, he moved to Mankato, Minnesota, and had a tailoring and dry-cleaning business. We met in Minnesota. In 1940, we drove out to New York City to tell his family goodbye—we were moving to California.

Roy Rogers: Nudie wasn't at it very long until practically everybody knew it. He was a hit right away. There weren't too many of them wearing fancy clothes at that time. A lot of them thought it was too loud, but I was on the road night after night, and you had to have new, different kinds of things. It made a lot of difference in your entrance. And the kids liked it if I had different little things on the clothes. I kept getting into it pretty heavy. The clothes were all mine. The studio had certain clothes that I wore in my pictures, but the other clothes were mine. I paid for them. Almost every shirt has a different kind of design on it. I don't know how much is too much, but we made some wild ones. As soon as I'd get an idea for a suit, he'd make it for me. There's one shirt with a little Indian girl on the back of it. I had that made because we'd adopted a little Indian girl. And then there's one with Bullet, my dog, on it. His people could just paint any picture with a sewing machine.

We drove the whole way to Los Angeles, staying in little motels and bungalows. In California, Nudie started with a business that contracted to make Western shirts. We were living in a loft above a five-and-dime on Hollywood Boulevard. It was called the Frontier Shirt Company. He made his own patterns. There were so many Western bands and Western clubs at that time.

Hank Snow *(Canadian country singer):* I started wearing fancy stage costumes in the fifties. I got all my costume ideas just by walking into Nudie's store. That was all I needed to see. I was very specific about how I wanted the costumes to look. The tailor and I would get together and exchange ideas, but mainly I would tell the tailor what I wanted. The clothes are fifty percent of anybody's act. Anybody in show business can vouch for that.

Hank Thompson: In 1948, I came out and worked for six weeks at the Riverside Rancho. That's where I met Nudie. Tex Williams was playing there. I saw the outfits he had on, and I knew they weren't Turk's. I asked Tex where they got these outfits, and he said, "There's a little Jewish man who lives out in the Valley, and he and his wife have a place in their garage, and they made these up for me." Nudie came out to see us and liked our music and told us that if we'd go pick out the material and buy it, he could make us up suits for a lot less money than Turk was charging. So I was the second one that Nudie ever made clothes for.

I went out there and we got acquainted, and he made outfits for me and my band for years and years. All those things with rhinestones and bright colors. He did things like the "Humpty Dumpty" suit, and he made some suits with airplanes on them, because I flew my own plane. And there were suits with ducks and deer on them, for hunting. Really pretty suits with things that were special to me.

Once I was working the **Golden Nugget,** and he made me a suit that had a **pot of gold and all the GOLD nuggets** up the sleeves. It was covered in rhinestones and embroidery. It was so heavy. I'd go in and get four or five suits at a time. You had to have a varied wardrobe because you played the same places a lot. One of the band members made notes of what we wore, so that when we went back, we wouldn't wear the same thing. The band's outfits were all the same, but not the real extensive rhinestone thing.

Bobbie Cohen: While Nudie was recuperating from a hernia operation, he decided to go for the Western market. He liked the people in the industry—the rodeos and the horse shows and all the country & Western singers. We bought a house in the Valley, and Nudie brought in a table-tennis table and set up shop in the garage. He called the business Nudie's Rodeo Tailors. He was always sorry he used the word "rodeo."

Meanwhile, Tex Williams had a band called the Western Caravan. He was working in the Palace Barn nightclub. Nudie set up a booth in the Palace Barn. Tex would plug him a lot. In the early days, it cost $17.50 for Western pants and a shirt. A suit and coat cost $75.

Eddie Dean: Tex Williams was responsible for Nudie, in a way. Tex had a horse, and he sold it to give the money to Nudie to start the business.

Buck Owens: I started wearing fancy costumes in 1960. I'd had a good record, and I went down to Nudie's and bought two costumes. One was lavender, a Western-cut suit, with buckles on the false pockets at the waist and on the front. The other was exactly the same, but it was a watermelon color. I paid $125 for those first suits I had made at Nudie's. They'd have the bolts of cloth there, and you'd pick the color. There were times when I gave away a suit without even wearing it, because after the suit was made, the color wasn't the same as it looked on the bolt of cloth.

Manuel: When I was no older than ten, I walked five miles to see *Lone Ranger* episodes. Later, I made his mask. Whenever they ask me who was the most exciting person to work for, it was him—the Lone Ranger.

Marty Stuart: Nudie had a way of promoting himself, of getting a lot of publicity. I was aware that he was the guy who made those suits. He found a few people who were really worth suiting great, like Carl Smith, Ray Price, Roy Rogers, Rex Allen. He seemed to make those guys his calling cards. When I finally went to California the first time, it was 1973 and I was thirteen years old, on a trip with Lester Flatt. I had somebody take me to Nudie's. Nudie was really nice to me because I played the mandolin, and Nudie played the mandolin. We played a little, then Manuel came in, and we just immediately hit it off. I asked him about a suit. He said, "They're about $2,500. If you save your money and have some hits, you can have one some day." He gave me a shirt that day. He cut it down so it would fit me. It was white with red piping and red flowers. I went away just beaming. I felt like I was in heaven there, all those suits hanging there and all those boots. I saw the men who sewed and the boot makers as real artists. I saw Nudie as the big star and these guys as the sidemen in the band.

Manuel: I apprenticed to a tailor at six or seven. I was blessed with an interesting job. Your parents throw you this. The tailor was a nice man. I never wasted any time. It takes fifteen years to get to be a master tailor. When I started, fad fashion didn't exist. There was the style of each state in Mexico. I was making prom dresses for the teenage girls. You could make a beautiful girl look dashing. You're born this way–it's not something you can learn. I thought, "Wow, what you can do with cloth!" Then I went to Argentina because it was the top of fashion. I still didn't care for the classic dressage of men. I'd wear a red sleeve and a blue sleeve and conchas for buttons. I was the strangest human being in my little town. The interest the women had in me was the greatest thing. I came to the U.S. when I was twenty-one. When I went to Nudie's, it was to sew shirts and pants. I was a peacock. I always dressed up. Nudie said that when I went there for a job, he thought I wouldn't want to work in the mess of the shop. He cleaned off a machine for me to sit down to work. I was with Nudie for fourteen years. I really never saw Nudie sit at the sewing machine or cut fabric or design. I did all the cars, all the Pontiacs.

Roy "Dusty" Rogers, Jr. *(son of Roy Rogers):* It seemed like Dad was always stopping by Nudie's, whether it was for a cup of coffee or a fitting. Nudie was like a big uncle to me. He'd stuff a donut in my mouth when I'd come along with my dad.

Roy Rogers: In the early forties, we had a clothes store. I had a lot of commercial tie-ins, and I thought it would be nice to have a place near the studio. People out on the road were asking, "Who made your shirts, and where could we get one?" I thought it would be a good thing. It wasn't.

Bobbie Cohen: For Hank Thompson, Nudie decided to make a horseshoe pocket, and that became one of his signatures. Webb Pierce had so many hits, and he'd get a suit made for each new one. For "There Stands the Glass," Nudie made Webb a suit with wine pouring out of a glass. He made costumes in extreme styles for the performers. He toned them down for the general public.

Marty Stuart: When we were living in Mississippi when I was a kid, all the country stars had syndicated TV shows out of Nashville. **The one that really stuck out was Ernest Tubb's.** He was a great-looking cowboy with a white hat. His band could really play, and they had matching uniforms down to their belt buckles and boots.

One time, **Ernest Tubb** came to play our fair in Mississippi. A green bus pulled up, and it said in big letters on the side, *Ernest Tubb and the Texas Troubadours, Stars of the Grand Ole Opry and Decca Records.* Man, those guys started stepping off that bus in those suits, and that old man came out in his hat, and it just tore me apart.

Of course, the king of all that stuff was Porter Wagoner. He had a variety show, and the entrance to his show was really dramatic. You would hear a door open, and the camera followed these boot heels, walking from the dressing room to the studio. And the boot heels were covered in rhinestones. When the camera went up his leg—and he was a really tall guy—it showed this fascinating suit. And his band was all decked out.

Carrot Top Anderson: *Ranch Party* was a take-off on and had all my cast from *Town Hall Party*. We had a terrific cast—Johnny Bond, Tex Ritter, Joe and Rose Lee Maphis, Wesley and Marilyn Tuttle. During the six and a half years we did the show, we had every person in the business on the show. **I gave a lot of people their first break, like Jim Reeves, Johnny Horton, and the Collins Kids.**

Larry Collins *(younger brother of Lorrie Collins and guitarist of the Collins Kids):* We were born in Tulsa, Oklahoma. Lorrie would always sing in church, and my parents took her to California to see if she had a shot at making something of herself. The feedback was good, so that next Christmas, they got me a guitar, and we all moved to L.A. I was about seven. While they were working on Lorrie, trying to get something going, I was in my room or in the garage practicing my guitar, **an old STELLA guitar that my parents had borrowed money from the bank to buy.**

In 1954, my sister Lorrie and I decided to go to an amateur contest at the town hall in Compton. We entered as the **Collins Kids**. It was our first show together, and we won. **They hired us for the TV show, *Town Hall Party.*** At first, they had a Friday and Saturday night TV show, then it was just Saturday night, for three hours, from ten until one. They threw a fit about us kids being on so late, until we got permission from the courts. They didn't want kids working after ten. Until we got permission from the judge, they opened the show with us singing, in the middle of a song, so we got away with it.

Marilyn Tuttle *(singer and cast member of* Ranch Party*):* Spade Cooley was the first to have a show on the radio with country & Western dance music. Spade was a little tiny guy. Foreman Phillips had the first country & Western show on TV, in 1950. We were on six days a week, three hours a day. There was a rule that you couldn't repeat a number for three weeks. There was Merle Travis, Johnny Bond, Tex Ritter, a big group of us. Liberace was just starting then, and he was on a stage right beside ours. It was so many hours that we just all wore out after a year. Then the promoter Bill Wagnon secured the town hall in Compton and chose the cast for *Town Hall Party*. We were on every Friday and Saturday night. It was live TV; there aren't even any tapes or kinescopes of those old shows.

Rose Lee and Joe Maphis with the Collins Kids; the inimitable Lefty Frizzell

Wesley Tuttle *(guitarist and singer):* *Town Hall Party* started on local TV in L.A. in 1951. I was the music director, in charge of the sound. I'd be up in the booth, adjusting levels, and when it was time for me to do a song, I'd run down from the booth to the stage. *Town Hall Party* had **Johnny Cash** and **Lefty Frizzell** **there a lot,** and Merle Travis and Tex Ritter. I remember this one time, Johnny Cash came to the show. He'd been playing from Shreveport to California. He walked in carrying his guitar. Then his manager came in carrying the guitar case. I couldn't figure it out, why he didn't have the guitar in the case. Then I saw them open it later, and it was full of money. That was how they carried the money they made back then.

When we decided to do *Ranch Party* in 1955, it was basically the same cast as *Town Hall Party*, but Tex Ritter was the host and it was syndicated nationally. We filmed a whole bunch of shows at once. We had to wear the same clothes all the time, so they could cut up the film and make thirty-nine episodes. We booked in guests who were famous, too. **Patsy Cline was on. She was very hard and aloof.**

Rose Lee Maphis: The *Ranch Party* cast made quite a few tours up through Canada. We toured with Tex Ritter and the Collins Kids and everyone. I had so much respect and admiration for Tex Ritter. If I were sitting in a room and he walked in, I felt like I should stand up. He was a fascinating man to talk to. The best time for us to tour Canada was the winter time, and we'd do these big shows in ice-hockey arenas. The people would sit in chairs on the ice! **It was so cold,** it was hard to perform.

Wesley Tuttle: Tex Ritter was murder to tour with. He had to stop and read every roadside marker. I worked on one of Ritter's recording sessions, and that's when Capitol signed me, too. Their first artist was Jack "Oklahoma" Guthrie, Tex Ritter was the second, and then me. We got a flat rate in the contract. A couple of years later, we also got a half a cent a record. We played maybe six or eight songs in one session. The band knew the song, and we just did the arrangements on the spot.

The cast of Town Hall Party; a rare snapshot of Patsy Cline

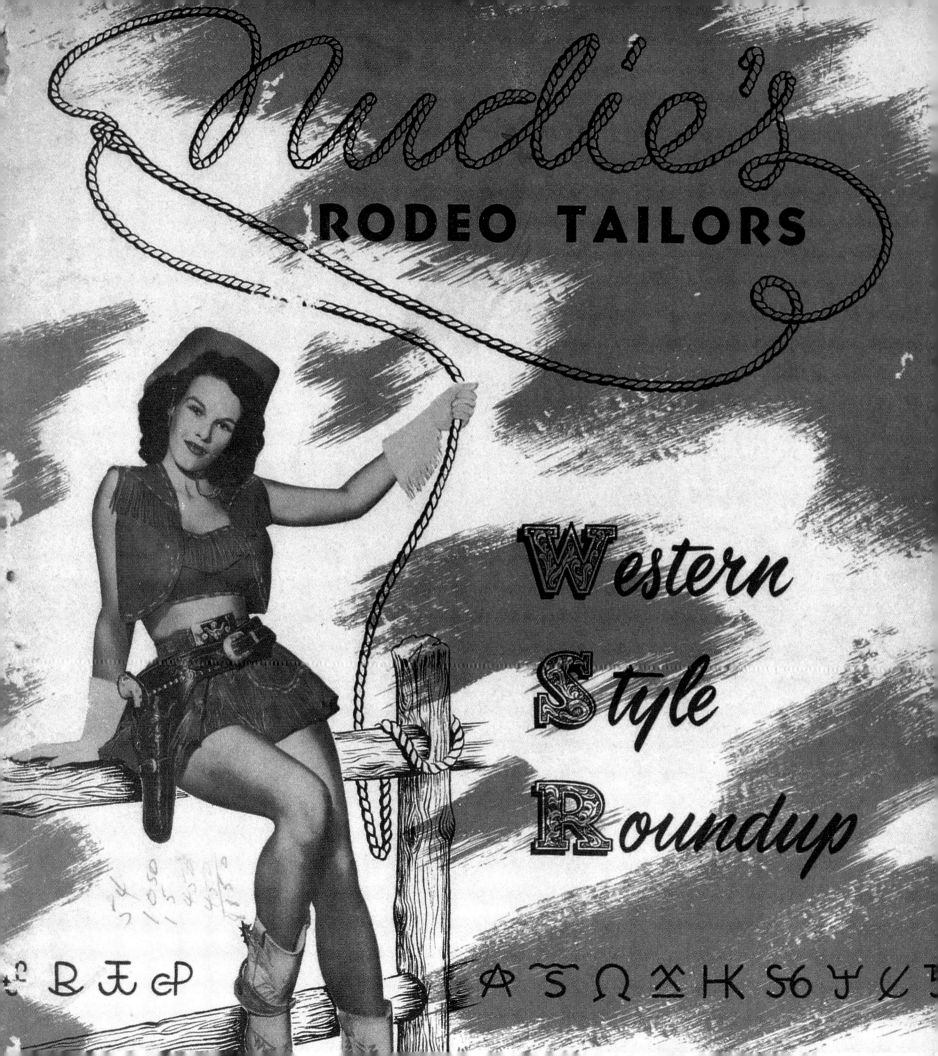

Larry Collins: The show *Town Hall Party* sent Lorrie to charm school. She used to walk around with a book on her head. We were two kids from Oklahoma, and it happened to us so fast, from living on the farm to having a weekly TV show to playing 26,000 people at Madison Square Garden. We were on a bill with Rin Tin Tin. We were the musical act, then they had a big thing with the cavalry and Rin Tin Tin. We were second-billed to the dog. About six or seven months after we appeared on *Town Hall Party*, we got a recording contract with Columbia Records. We were just doing high-energy country & Western with a beat. **Then they started calling us ROCKABILLY.**

Buck Owens: I own one of Nudie's old custom cars. It's a Pontiac convertible with guns for door handles, guns on the fenders. It's a club coupe, with a saddle between the front two seats. There are silver dollars all over the dash. In 1976, I went in to the shop. He told me to park in back, and when I pulled in there, he had two of those cars. You could tell one was brand new, and the other was two or three years old. I said, "You've got two of them now." Nudie said, "I just had one made, and I'm trying to sell the other one." I said, "What do you want for it?" And he said, "$11,000." I wrote him the check right then. I've had the car ever since. If somebody offered me $100,000 for it, I'd think about it. That's all I'd do, is think about it. I wouldn't sell it.

Rose Clements *(embroiderer for Nudie Cohen):* I did all of the embroidery at Nudie's from the sixties on. I was the only one. One night, I was watching TV, and Nudie was on and he was showing his suits, and I thought, "My God, I can do that." I called him up, and I started work for him right away. I'd never worked on costumes before Nudie. There are two different embroidery machines and I combine the two, so it looks custom. One is satin stitch, like a monogram machine. The other is chain stitch, or hand-guided. What has brought the Nudie look back? Fashion goes in circles. But the young ones coming up don't want the cornier stuff. **It's gotten refined since the day of suits with big alligators on them.**

Marty Stuart: I love what took place out in California. All my influences came out of there, from the way I dress to the way I play guitar. It's called a West Coast sound. That West Coast thing just rings true in my heart. Play a Buck Owens record from 1960, and play a Carl Smith record from that same year. You can hear the difference yourself: Owens' is just a little edgier, a bit looser, has a little more rhythm. I call it more of a Saturday-night sound, more danceable, more honky-tonk than a crooner thing. **If you had a little edge on you, if you had a little cowboy on you, if you were a bit of an innovator or a wildcat,** you could stand a chance of making it more in California than in Nashville.

Larry Collins: By 1955, we were wearing the fancy clothes. Nudie did most of the outfits for the entertainers on *Town Hall Party*. He made our first suits, designed them and picked out the colors. I think the first colors were lavender, yellow, and red. Mine had little red guitars on it and long red fringe. **Nudie was an artist.** You couldn't believe what he came up with. He'd give us choices, like, did we want horses or guitars in the design? We used to go to his shop on Lankershim and take our guitars. He played the mandolin, and we'd play together while they worked on our suits. They also made our cowboy boots. They always matched the outfit. Even then, the whole outfit would cost $500 to $1,000. **To do that high-energy ROCKABILLY called for the WILD CLOTHES. They were just as important as the music.**

Nudie and his Mandolin

Includes over sixty never before published pictures of Nudie and his friends.

Carrot Top Anderson: About the same time as I started *Town Hall Party*, I had a live show in San Francisco, another in Phoenix, one in Salt Lake, and then I was back in L.A. for shows on Saturday and Sunday. In 1952, from January until November, I flew 100,000 miles and put 75,000 miles on my automobile. Then I went to the hospital with a nervous-exhaustion breakdown. In 1961, I left the business altogether. My part of the business was dying, and rock & roll was taking a strong hold. I quit before I had to go back down the ladder, winding up in juke joints with a bunch of drunks.

Marty Stuart: In the mid-seventies, the hillbillies were wearing Nudie suits around the Opry, the cowboys were wearing them on the movie sets, and **the BYRDS, the BURRITO BROTHERS, and the DEAD** were wearing them, too. The rockers were embracing that old country tradition in the middle of hanging out with the Rolling Stones. A lot of these guys came out of the folk boom, playing acoustic music, and they'd plugged in when Dylan had. After they plugged in, they'd made their rock & roll hits, but eventually their roots had to show.

Gram Parsons, for instance, the Burritos' guitarist, was a Florida guy who grew up on George Jones and bluegrass and old Lefty Frizzell and Merle Haggard. **He probably watched the same PORTER WAGONER shows that I did. And I'm sure he was a *Grand Ole Opry* fan.** If you check out his old albums, he was singing George Jones and Louvin Brothers songs. And when he wasn't writing stuff that resembled that world, he was covering their old stuff. Looking back at the major country-rock players–Gram Parsons, Emmylou Harris, Clarence White, Chris Hillman, Roger McGuinn–all of those guys started out playing acoustic music, bluegrass, or folk, and most of them have gone back to their original roots.

 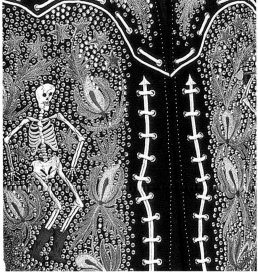

Clarence White, the guitar star of the Byrds, was my guitar hero. He had all of his clothes made at Nudie's. **He carried a bit of that old cowboy style, but he had a rock & roll flair.** I liked the fact that all the cowboy rockers were wearing Nudie clothes. I saw them as country-rock clothes. Manuel was still at Nudie's, and he was making hip-huggers for Gram Parsons that had marijuana leaves and pills and naked ladies. It was true rock & roll. John Lennon was in there, Dylan was in there. Elton John even. All the rock cats were in there, as well as John Wayne.

Rose Clements: I did a lot of clothes for Johnny Cash and Emmylou Harris. I did the logo of the Grateful Dead on suits for them. **That was a dilly.** George Harrison had a suit made, a red one, and he had me embroider his mantra around the collar: *Hare krishna, krishna, krishna.* Mick Jagger had a logo–the big lips with the tongue sticking out. He wanted a T-shirt embroidered, but not the tongue, something else in the lips, you know? I wouldn't do it. **I must be the only one that refused Mick Jagger.**

Seminal country-rock figure Gram Parsons on the cover of the posthumous release, Sleepless Nights; *Day of the Dead jacket by Manuel for Marty Stuart*

Manuel: I opened my own shop in Hollywood in 1974. There was nothing in it but a tin plate for cigarettes and a little rug. One day somebody comes through the door with a paper bag. It was Freddy Hart, and the bag had $10,000 in it. He said, "You buy what you need, and I want to order six suits." Johnny Cash called the next week. He said, "You make my clothes. Why didn't you call me to tell me you'd left Nudie's?" Then Buck Owens, Ray Price, and Jimmy Dickens called. It was like they'd all gotten together.

One day, I got a call from Turk. He was closing his shop. I said, "I would love to have all your machinery and all your fabrics and linings." I went over there and bought all of Turk's shop. I said, "I'll pay you whatever you want." I bought all the black heads, the old Singers, and old, broken, embroidery machines. I said, **"I want your scissors."** I said, "I'll give you my check, you add everything up, and you put the value on the check." **He took the check, and he never cashed it.**

Marty Stuart: The first piece I had in the costume collection was a suit owned by George Jones. The story about how I got it is really strange. Somehow or other, I inherited a pair of Hank Williams Sr.'s gloves. It was a pair of black, fringed Nudie gloves, that had the initials HW on them. These were the most jinxed pair of gloves. Every time I would wear those gloves, my car wouldn't start, or the handle would fall off my guitar case. I could salute and break my neck. They had the damnedest aura. I was at a point where I thought these are the coolest things in the world, but I'm afraid to keep them in the house. Waylon had a pair of Hank's boots that he said he could wear to a session and things would go nuts. One night he had those boots on, and a tree fell on his car.

I ran into Johnny Rodriguez one night, and I was telling him these stories, and he said, "Do you want to get rid of them?" I said, "What have you got?" He said, "I've got a cool George Jones suit." So he got Hank's gloves, and I got George's suit.

If you're having a conversation before a show, you say, "Excuse me, but I've got to get my hillbilly suit on." It's a lick. I've always loved it. I understand why it offended the old cats. It was used against them in New York or L.A. where "hillbilly" meant country-hayseed-cousin. There's still a little bit of that.

Hillbilly means you encompass the roots of country & Western, which takes in bluegrass, folk, gospel, blues, all of that. **It's a bit edgier and a little more raucous.** It's more exciting. It has a lot of good cousins: rock & roll, rockabilly. It's a neat way to play country music validly. **HILLBILLY** means, if you're looking at things from a roots tradition, **the picture is a whole lot richer.**

Nathan Turk, an unsung hero of American design; Manuel Cuevas, the consummate Nashville tailor. Many of the costumes credited to Nudie because they bear the label of his shop were actually designed and tailored by Manuel during his years working there.

DESIGNED FOR:
Johnny Cash
manuel
OF CALIFORNIA
DESIGNED FOR:
Sally Kellerman
manuel
OF CALIFORNIA
DESIGNED FOR:
Roy Clark
Conway Twitty

The Maddox Brothers onstage: bassist Fred Maddox was the leader of the act; Don played the fiddle; and Cal played guitar. The raucous sound and ribald lyrics of the Maddoxes' music helped pave the way for rockabilly. The whole family worked as fruit pickers when they first moved to California, and after they made it, they performed in towns around California where migrant workers came to hear them. That may explain the grapes on these suits Turk made for the Maddoxes in a cream-colored gabardine. Rose liked to say these outfits were made for them when they were booked to play a cast party for the movie, *The Grapes of Wrath*. Probably not, it turned out, but it was a good story.

In 1949, Jimmy Wakely was so popular that he beat out both Frank Sinatra and Bing Crosby in *Billboard's* "favorite pop vocalist" poll. He grew up on a ranch in Oklahoma and was discovered by Gene Autry, who brought him to California to appear on his *Melody Ranch* radio show. Wakely's 1948 hit, "One Has My Name, the Other Has My Heart" started a whole cycle of songs that we now think of as the basic country & Western theme: cheating. **Standing in a fruit-covered suit** with his band by his bus, Hank Snow, from Nova Scotia, was known at first as the Yodeling Ranger, though he was never actually a ranger. He could yodel, however, and his first RCA sides in 1934 were "Lonesome Blue Yodel" and "Prisoned Cowboy." He wrote his own big hit, "I'm Moving On," which went to number one in 1950.

Variations on a theme: Western shirts. Middle row, farthest right, is a design by Nathan Turk that became a standard Western look, with pearl buttons at the cuff, leather lacings instead of buttons at the neck, and "smile" pockets with arrowheads. Manuel's modern recreation of the same look is just below it. **Hank Thompson** wears a shirt Nudie Cohen made for him to celebrate his big hit, "Humpty Dumpty Heart." As a swing-band leader whose influence extended even to country-rock, Thompson also penned such chart hits as the wonderfully titled, "The Next Time I Fall in Love, I Won't." It must be footnoted that Thompson had one of the most amicable trades in pop-music history: he and guitar great Merle Travis actually divorced their own wives and then married each other's.

Earl Scott, an unknown, wears a jacket covered in Scottie dogs. Having the singer's name tied to the design was a signature Nudie Cohen trick. **Ferlin Husky** wears a Nudie jacket that features dog sleds on the sleeves and husky dogs on the front. Husky first made a name for himself—a completely different name—as Terry Preston, dueting with Jean Shepard on the hit, "A Dear John Letter." Another novelty song, "I Feel Better All Over," introduced him, again, as Ferlin Husky. And then he recorded a couple of sides as someone named Simon Crum. His biggest record was "On the Wings of a Dove." Happy to overwork the dog metaphor, Husky's band was called the Hush Puppies.

Roy Rogers reads the new issue of his comic book to a boy in an iron lung. Not even polio could keep Roy from his fans, or the photographers from Roy. **At right,** Roy is dressed up to show off a new disc for the Viewmaster, a fifties toy that clicked the reel around to tell a story photo by photo. Both pictures are promoting spin-off products of the popular Roy Rogers character. Not only were there the Dell Comics, there was a whole series of Whitman books, with titles like *Dwarf-Cattle Ranch* and *Snowbound Outlaws*, and paper dolls, with lots of fancy cowboy clothes to cut out. And that was just the tip of the promotional iceberg: there were lamps, boots, lunch boxes, holster sets, guitars, guns, watches, and pocket knives featuring the King of the Cowboys on the rearing Trigger. All are more than worth their weight in plastic today.

The Maddox Brothers and Rose in the late forties with an expanded line-up that included Bud Duncan, second from left, and next to him, guitar player Jimmy Winkle. In Johnny Whiteside's authorized biography of Rose, he says Winkle and Rose fell in love. Whiteside writes in *Ramblin' Rose*, "The image of Rose and Jimmy as chaste sweethearts offers a strange and touching tableau: the splendor of their Turk uniforms glimmering in the darkness as they rolled up Highway 99, the slight flush of excitement and affection, the low whispers punctuated by the occasional sharp inquiry from Lula, her two-cents' worth being tossed at the lovers regardless of their interest in it. For the moment, Rose was happy." **The Buckaroos,** in the short jacket style the Maddoxes favored, line up beside Buck Owens. In the early sixties, Owens toured with Rose.

Honky-tonk singer **Carl Butler** and his wife Pearl were a popular sixties act. Their first recording together, "Cross Over," made Carl give up his solo act and stick to the marital duet. They also appeared together in a single movie, the weirdly titled, cheatin'-sounding, *Second Fiddle to a Steel Guitar*. These hilariously detailed Nudie costumes, covered in burros and sombreros, probably commemorated their chart single, "Little Pedro." **The detail of this parade scarf** from Nudie's shows the extent to which the embroiderers could paint a picture in rhinestones and chain-stitching. This scarf was draped over the horse, behind the saddle, as part of the elaborate outfit worn by horse and rider in parades or rodeo entrances.

Rose Lee Maphis and her guitar-hero husband, Joe Maphis, sign autographs. The couple met in 1948 on *The Old Dominion Barn Dance* out of Richmond, Virginia; the country & Western radio variety shows were popular all over the country and not just in the West or Southwest. They married and headed to California, where they became stalwarts on *Town Hall Party*. Joe, who played fiddle, guitar, banjo, mandolin, and bass, was also known for his studio sessions with Ricky Nelson, then a teen idol. Recently, Rose Lee worked in the costume department at the Opry.

PAGES

4 2 - 53

The Collins Kids were rocking country pioneers. They played innocent, exuberant rockabilly songs like "Soda Poppin' Around" and "Beetle Bug Boogie." Larry Collins often played a twin-necked Mosrite guitar, like his guitar tutor, Joe Maphis. Lorrie eventually married Johnny Cash's manager, and Larry went on to cowrite "You're the Reason God Made Oklahoma" and "Delta Dawn." They still get together to appear at popular rockabilly shows in Europe. **Teddy and Doyle Wilburn** first appeared on Missouri street corners as part of the Wilburn Family act. By the forties, the Wilburn Brothers were part of the Decca roster, with Ray Whitley, Ernest Tubb, and the Patsys—Montana and Cline. They later had a TV show and founded a Nashville talent agency.

Nathan Turk's suits for the Maddox Brothers and Rose served them for their many public appearances from the forties through the fifties. They played live radio shows, as pictured here, as well as concerts. They even played places like Crawford's Market in El Monte, a big grocery store that opened in 1938 at a busy street intersection. Crawford's sponsored many country & Western nights, with acts like the Maddox Brothers and Rose, just to draw people out to the market. They also had giant chunks of cheese and enormous cartons of milk, in case the music wasn't enough. The live radio shows, of course, didn't require the fancy clothes, but the Maddoxes were usually photographed under the station's call letters after the show, so they wore them anyway.

Little Jimmy Dickens was nicknamed Tater after he scored a Top Ten record in 1949 with the bizarrely titled, "Take an Old Cold Tater and Wait." Not that it was the strangest song he would record: that was his smash crossover hit in 1965, "May the Bird of Paradise Fly up Your Nose." Because he's known for the novelty songs, it's a surprise to hear the pure rockabilly boogie of his early Columbia sides, like "Hillbilly Fever"and "Rockin' with Red." **Fashion note: Roy Rogers** appears to be wearing a chiffon bandana in this publicity still from his TV-show days in the fifties. Nudie Cohen made this dazzling shirt, covered in embroidered German shepards as a tribute to Bullet. Today the dog is stuffed and barking up a silent storm in a diorama at the Roy Rogers & Dale Evans Museum in Victorville, California—a must for cowboy fans.

After mastering the steel guitar, Les "Carrot Top" Anderson was first a Texas Playboy with Bob Wills in 1940, then fronted his own band, the Melody Wranglers. He later became the lead vocalist with Spade Cooley's swing band, the "house band" at the Santa Monica Ballroom. Starting out, Clelland Irving "Red" Anderson sang in his church choir in Arkansas; it was Wills who changed Red's name to Les, and Spade who changed Les's name to Carrot Top. On old 78 RPM records by Spade Cooley for RCA, Carrot Top Anderson is often the lead vocalist. Still wearing the suits covered in the little carrot man that he'd worn with Cooley's act, Carrot Top was also a popular singer in the *Town Hall Party* and *Ranch Party* casts.

Alvis Edgar Owens, nicknamed Buck, moved to Bakersfield, California, in 1951. Having played guitar on sessions with such noisy Elvis descendants as Wanda Jackson and Faron Young, Buck himself got signed to Capitol Records in 1957. Owens and his rollicking band, the Buckaroos, delivered their music loud and fast to a dancing bar audience. In true maverick form, he called one of his albums, *Buck 'Em!* **Is there anyone cooler than the young George Jones,** pictured here in a Nudie suit and slick two-toned boots? He scored his first number-one song with "White Lightning" in 1959. Jones also made a famous partnership with wife and future ex-wife Tammy Wynette. Many of his songs have been covered by artists as far afield as Elvis Costello, drawn to the heart-choking lyrics in classic numbers like "She Thinks I Still Care" and "Good Year for the Roses."

Hank Thompson demonstrates how you can maintain a pompadour and wear a cowboy hat at the same time. The rhinestone-studded kerchief was *de rigueur*. Carrot Top Anderson's kerchiefs were made-to-order, like his outfits, and embroidered with the carrot man. A similar embroidered and rhinestone-studded kerchief costs $35 today at Manuel's, the Nashville tailoring shop. In 1998, Curb Records released a Hank Thompson tribute album that featured guest stars like Lyle Lovett, George Jones, and Vince Gill. **How could Carl and Pearl Butler** have failed to notice that they would clash with the wallpaper? In rhinestone-covered Nudie suits, the Butlers smile here for a fan's snapshot. Carl had a small hit called "Honky Tonkitis," a condition like the boogie-woogie flu, but didn't have a number-one record till he dueted with Pearl.

Rose at the microphone, between her brothers Henry and Cal. **The folk-art motif** on the suits suggests Turk's ties to his native Poland. The Maddoxes often took the jackets off because of the California heat, so Turk made the shirts, in satins the color of some of the embroidery trim, as showy and intricately designed as the jackets.

PAGES 58-69

Outside the Jones Music Company, which would have carried the sheet music to his latest hit, Wesley Tuttle signs autographs, dressed in a fancy Turk suit. Though he'd lost all but the thumb and little finger on his left hand in an accident when he was six, Wesley Tuttle was already an accomplished guitarist by age thirteen. He begged his parents to drive him to Hollywood to audition for the Saturday-morning radio show, *The Lucky Stars*. Yodeling and picking, Tuttle joined the show every Saturday afterward. When he started recording, his record company made him hold a plastic hand in publicity photos and in the film clips of the pre-MTV era called Snaderscopes, which were like early music videos.

A plethora of shirts designed by Nathan Turk in Marty Stuart's priceless collection of Rose Maddox's trend-setting costumes. They were carried on hangers on a rod in the back seat of the touring Cadillacs and only cleaned by one dry cleaner in Hollywood whenever the band came off the road. The dress with the magnolia design on gray gabardine was also part of Rose's wardrobe and was worn by her on one of her album covers. **In 1957, Rose Maddox** left her brothers' act and went solo. Known as the Sweetheart of Hillbilly Swing, Rose toured with Merle Haggard, Wynn Stewart, and Buck Owens, with whom she had a hit record in 1961 called "Loose Talk." At the time, she was the top female country singer in the country.

Detail of a classic Nathan Turk shirt design. **Lefty Frizzell,** in a rare snapshot taken backstage by a fan, wears a similar shirt by Nudie. *The Los Angeles Times'* peerless music critic Robert Hilburn wrote in a review of a compilation, "Frizzell was arguably the greatest male singer in post-World War II country music—yes, even more influential than Hank Williams, his main honky-tonk rival in the early 1950s." In the same piece, Merle Haggard is quoted as saying about Lefty, "To my mind, he had a greater voice than Elvis....Every breath was authentic." His first record, "If You've Got the Money, I've Got the Time," was a hit in 1950. A great songwriter, as well as an innovative and much imitated singer, Frizzell had four singles in the Top Ten in 1951. Even the Band covered one of his songs, "Long Black Veil," on their stunning debut, *Music from Big Pink*.

Spade Cooley died in 1959, released from prison before his life term for stomping his wife to death was over. He appears as a raging, jealous maniac in Elmore Leonard's *Hollywood Nocturne*. Born Donell Clyde Cooley, he was nicknamed Spade, because of his dark skin, and then, in an era of ghastly political incorrectness, he was referred to as "the Neutered Chinese" (spade or *spayed*). In his happy, pre-murdering days, his popular band, the Western Swing Dance Gang, was one of the biggest aggregations that performed at dances, sometimes swelling to twenty-four musicians on stage. But talk about ironies: his biggest hit was called, prophetically, "Shame on You." **Music symbols grace** both Cooley's Turk suit and the red one at left, made for Cal Maddox by Turk, which has music notes running down the entire length of the pants leg.

Clockwise from upper left corner: Gene Autry hugs the Collins Kids, proving some laid-back singers could embrace the rockabilly acts; Bonnie Lou Okum signs fans' notes; a line of gussied-up country & Western singers backstage at the civic center in Butte, Montana, includes Hank Snow (third from left) and Slim Whitman, of the late-night commercials (second from right); Gene Autry with a boy in a wheelchair; a handsome young Waylon Jennings squeezes toward Dolly Parton and Porter Wagoner, who toured together; the Maddoxes meet Wesley and Marilyn Tuttle; Little Jimmy Dickens, Nudie favorite Judy Lynn, and Ernest Tubb; Webb Pierce stands backstage with a promoter in a card suit (Nudie dressed not just performers but people who worked in other parts of the music business); and a young Porter Wagoner backstage. Inset: one Nudie suit meets another.

One of the earliest pictures of Fred, Rose, and Cal Maddox, after they arrived in California but before they could afford Turk outfits. The photo is from Rose's own scrapbook and was probably taken by Lula Maddox, who was still obviously fascinated by the California flora. Cacti like that were an inspiration and a thematic Western design element to the likes of Nathan Turk. Many of the brothers' pants were flourished with cactus branches at the bottom. **A pair of pants** from a suit designed for singer Carl Butler by Turk. The chain-stitched green cactus creeps up the leg of the gold gabardine pants. The jacket that went with it, pictured in detail on the title page, is bursting with big, blooming, red desert flowers and multicolored rhinestones.

Spade Cooley's band plays one of Foreman Phillips' barn dances. Radio shows would broadcast live from these dances, and later, live television broadcasts, like the local Los Angeles show *Town Hall Party*, caught the action. By the late fifties, country stalwarts had flown the coop, and the show featured rock pioneers like Eddie Cochran and Gene Vincent and their rockabilly bands. **Tex Ritter** was the host of *Ranch Party* and a featured performer on *Town Hall Party*. Woodward Maurice Ritter grew up on the Gulf Coast of Texas and studied voice at the University of Texas in Austin. He dropped out of law school and took on Hollywood, where he was nominated for an Academy Award for his singing of the theme song for *High Noon*.

Detail of one of the most beautiful and intricate Western shirts designed by Nathan Turk. **A similar design** is worn on a shirt by Jimmy Wakely, the singing cowboy and protégé of Gene Autry. Autry not only brought Wakely and his trio, which also featured Johnny Bond, to his radio show, he got Wakely into his pictures at Republic Studios. Wakely then got his own contract at rival studio Monogram and eventually made twenty-eight so-so Westerns as a singing cowboy. "Hollywood's indifference to folk material is not as irksome as its creation of fake folk songs to be nasalized, during a film's transitional passages, by an unseen darling of the night clubs," complained a critic of the singing-cowboy movie in an issue of *ABC-TV Hootenanny Show* magazine.

Lefty Frizzell models a watch. **In this extremely rare**, unpublished photo taken by a fan, Hank Williams, Sr. shows his sartorial side. In 1947, he had his first unforgettable, honky-tonking hit, "Lovesick Blues." Plagued by alcoholism, he died just five years later, at age twenty-nine, in the back of a car on New Year's Eve, having penned some of the greatest country songs ever written. In an early chapbook, Hank Williams wrote about songwriting: "You ask what makes our kind of music successful. I'll tell you. It can be explained in just one word: sincerity. When a hillbilly sings a crazy song, he feels crazy. When he sings, 'I laid my mother away,' he sees her a-laying right there in the coffin...He sings more sincere than most entertainers because the hillbilly was raised rougher than most entertainers. You got to have smelt a lot of mule manure before you can sing like a hillbilly."

Charline Arthur left her Texas home at sixteen to travel with a medicine show and became a a a star on Dallas's *Big D Jamboree*. Her man-troubled songs included "He Fiddled While I Burned" and "I'm Having a Party All by Myself." She passed away in obscurity in 1987, a bold, bluesy singer and a temperamental figure who was simply ahead of her time. In an interview quoted in her obituary, she said, "Wanda Jackson, Brenda Lee, and Patsy Cline all, in some way, patterned their styles after me. I was the first woman in country music to wear a slack suit onstage when all the other women were wearing those little gingham dresses. I was the first to break out of the Kitty Wells stereotype and boogie-woogie. I was shakin' that thing long before Elvis even thought about it." **Patsy Cline** snapped by a fan outside the Flame Cafe in Minneapolis. She died in a plane crash in 1963.

Detail of the back of the jacket worn by Cal Maddox in the fan's snapshot at right. This double-breasted jacket made for the Maddox Brothers is a style that took off after Hank Williams became popular. It was the look Williams favored, longer and a little more formal than what the Maddoxes had worn before. This costume shows tailor Nathan Turk at his best: the simple contrast of white on black, the lovely heart motif in the appliquéd design, the understated Western elements, like the arrowheads and the piping on the yoke, and the elegant lacing near the cuff on the sleeves. In their first week on the radio out of Modesto, California, playing a half-hour at 6:30 in the morning, the Maddoxes received over a thousand letters.

A singer in the Jimmie Rodgers tradition, Ernest Tubb's first big hit was the classic pacing-and-forgetting number, "Walkin' the Floor over You," which shot him to fame in 1942. With his band, the Texas Troubadours, he helped pioneer the honky-tonk style of country music that came out of the rowdy roadhouse bars of Texas. In the early forties, when jukeboxes were a fixture of beer halls, Tubb added electric guitar to make his band's records louder. Tubb complained to his record label, Decca, that he wanted "country & Western" not "hillbilly" as the category for his music in the company's record listings, starting a trend that hip young country artists have been reversing.

Emmylou Harris notably covered the Louvin Brothers' songs, as did the great young band Uncle Tupelo, which rocked and rolled through the Louvins' classic "Atomic Bomb," led by Jeff Tweedy. Ira and Charlie Louvin showed their gospel roots in preachy lyrics and sweet, close, high harmonies that were downright heavenly. Ira died in an auto accident at the height of their powers, but not before they'd released lovely duets like "If I Could Only Win Your Love" and "When I Stop Dreaming," and such scary sacred songs as "Satan Is Real." **In 1949, Stuart Hamblen** was so popular that a two-inch headline in *The Los Angeles Times* announced his conversion to Christianity: "Stuart Hamblen Hits the Sawdust Trail." His conversion made a big name out of the young minister who'd just held his first revival meeting in L.A.—Billy Graham.

The classic girl's Western outfit, by Turk for Rose Maddox. On black gabardine, Turk worked out an elaborate flower design in chain-stitching that matched the embroidery work on her brother's suits. The pink blouse for Rose's ensemble, embroidered in the same pattern, is satin. The fringe on the split skirt and vest is leather, and the hems are spotted with rhinestones. Because Hollywood was first to toss some glitter on the figure of the dusty cowpoke, it's only fitting that it's also where Turk, who settled there to flee the ghettos of New York, first made cowboy clothes that really did sparkle.

The most expensive item ever ordered at Nudie's shop was for Elvis Presley: he paid over $10,000 for a 24-carat-gold lamé suit. Of course, it wasn't in the Nudie's Rodeo Tailors catalog. You could, however, order hats, boots, and suits just like your favorite Western singers'. **Patsy Montana** introduced "I Want to Be a Cowboy's Sweetheart" on *The National Barn Dance*, a radio show out of Chicago. The record sold a million copies in 1935. The quintessential yodeler, she was born Rubye Blevins in Hot Springs, Arkansas, in 1914. She might have gotten her name from her early association with film cowboy Monte Montana, though they weren't married. The band the Prairie Ramblers backed her up on the radio and on her records, until she moved to Los Angeles in 1952, where she often appeared in forgettable B-Westerns.

Renowned for his influential guitar style, Merle Travis (in upper-right corner) headed to California after World War II, when L.A.'s country & Western scene was taking off. A deft guitarist, he played in bands with many of the great singers of the era. As writer or cowriter of hits like "Sixteen Tons" and "Smoke, Smoke, Smoke," he was also praised for his songwriting skill, as well as for reworking Southern folk songs, like "John Henry," into the country lexicon. **Charlie and Margie Linville,** known as the Fiddlin' Linvilles. Later, Margie dyed her hair and morphed into Fiddlin' Kate. Charlie Linville, with Merle Travis and Wesley Tuttle, had a band called the Coon Hunters in 1944.

One of eleven children of a Mexican rancher, Manuel Cuevas first designed prom dresses for his friends in his Michoacan high school. By the late fifties, he was working in Nudie's shop, later marrying the boss's daughter. Manuel has dressed nearly everyone in the music business: he put Elvis in jumpsuits, made Johnny Cash "the man in black," and gave Dwight Yoakam his contemporary C&W look. He also created fashions for the Jacksons, the Beatles, Bob Dylan, John Lennon, the Rolling Stones, and Linda Ronstadt. **The labels** sewn in clothes at Nathan Turk's Van Nuys, California shop and Nudie's Rodeo Tailors in North Hollywood. In 1953, when Nudie Cohen converted to Christianity, he put a vest on the bare-chested girl who sat on the fence in the drawing on his label.

Faron Young was born in Shreveport and after a stint on *The Louisiana Hayride*, moved on to the *Opry*. His many hits, like "Live Fast, Love Hard, and Die Young," show him to be a pretty mainstream country act for such a dark and handsome Elvis type. He's probably best known for the hit he made of Willie Nelson's, "Hello, Walls." **Signed to a record contract** while still in his teens, Young had an early rockabilly hit in "Goin' Steady." Undeniably best in the genre was Elvis, here with an unidentified lucky girl, who first recorded at Sun Studios in Memphis in July 1954. In 1999, some unpublished documents from Presley's archives were auctioned. One letter reveals that in 1954, Elvis was looking for bookings in Chicago but got this rejection note back: "There are few outlets for hillbilly entertainers in this area around Chicago."

Detail of the Turk shirt worn at right by Fred Maddox. **In the forties,** radio broadcasts featuring the Maddoxes' crude musical blend of fruit-tramp's blues and heartfelt gospel would reach all of California, Oregon, Washington, Arizona, and Nevada. They first took the stage of *The Grand Ole Opry* in 1949, wearing the outlandishly colorful costumes made for them by Turk. Though their style was a raw delivery of joking, giddy songs like "You Won't Believe This," and "Sally, Let Your Bangs Down," their show was also known for all its slapstick horseplay onstage.

PAGES 106-117

Two jackets by Manuel for Marty Stuart. The costumes photographed in color for this book are just some examples of the vintage costumes in Stuart's collection, which numbers around three hundred outfits. It also includes guitars; hand-tooled boots, belts and pistol holsters; and bespoke cowboy hats. A virtuoso guitarist, Stuart left Johnny Cash's band and stepped into the spotlight as a solo performer in 1985. **At right:** detail of a "good luck" jacket made for Stuart in blue gabardine for the release of his *Tempted* album. Collaborating, Stuart and Manuel came up with symbols for the jacket: "We put horseshoes on it and a good card hand, a lucky roll of the dice, a pistol, a little luck from the cross, and a rose for some charm," says Stuart.

Johnny Cash in a heartbreakingly handsome pose at the Hollywood Bowl. Embraced by the rock world for his cool look, poetically clear lyrics, and driving band, Cash was somehow always able to stay popular with country fans, too. Like Elvis, he recorded at Sun Records, cutting "Cry, Cry, Cry" in 1955. In David McGee's Carl Perkins bio, *Go, Cat, Go!*, he describes how Sam Phillips defined Cash's sound: "Placing Cash's rugged, ragged baritone voice up front in the mix, he used tape delay to create a slapback echo on both the voice and Luther Perkins's 'boom-chicka' guitar stylings....Cash and Grant flailed and slapped an unwavering, lumbering rhythm support, evoking the unrelenting trundle of a locomotive burning down the rails." **This jacket of black gabardine** with black embroidery shows Manuel's typical treatment of Cash costumes.

1.

2.

4.

Cutting

5.

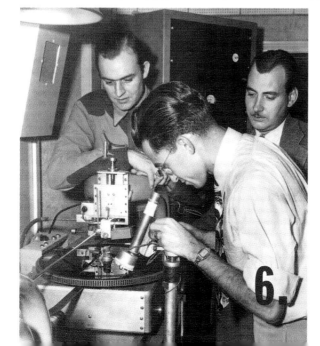

6.

a RECORD

with Wesley Tuttle

PHOTO credits

All color photographs of vintage costumes and record album covers by Kyle Ericksen.
5: Photo from *Hank Thompson, Folio of Favorite Recorded Hits*, published by the now defunct Metro-Music Publications. In the foreword, Hank thanks his wife, Dorothy, for the "splendid job she did taking, developing, and printing most of the photos" in the song book. **7:** Courtesy Thomas Sims Archives. **10:** Courtesy Wesley & Marilyn Tuttle. **12 & 13:** Thomas Sims Archives. **14 & 16** (Autry): Courtesy Hearst Newspaper Collection, Special Collections, University of Southern California Library, Los Angeles. **15-20** Thomas Sims Archives. **21 & 22:** Courtesy Manuel Cuevas. **23:** Courtesy MCA/Nashville; courtesy Reprise Records. **24-27:** Thomas Sims Archives. **29:** Courtesy Hank Thompson. **30 & 31:** Thomas Sims Archives. **32 & 33:** Hearst Newspaper Collection, USC Library. **34 & 35:** Thomas Sims Archives. **36:** Hearst Newspaper Collection, USC Library. **39-42:** Thomas Sims Archives. **44:** Courtesy Rose Lee Maphis. **46-51:** Thomas Sims Archives. **53:** Courtesy Les Anderson. **54:** Courtesy Doye O'Dell. **55-59:** Thomas Sims Archives. **60:** Hank Thompson. **61 & 62:** Thomas Sims Archives. **64:** Wesley & Marilyn Tuttle. **67-71:** Thomas Sims Archives. **72:** Hank Thompson. **73:** Thomas Sims Archives. **74:** Hearst Newspaper Collection, USC Library. **76-81:** Thomas Sims Archives. **83:** Hearst Newspaper Collection, USC Library. **84-87:** Thomas Sims Archives. **88 & 89:** Rose Lee Maphis; Thomas Sims Archives (Frizzell, Cline); Wesley & Marilyn Tuttle (*Town Hall Party* cast). **Cover & 90:** Courtesy Dottie Ethridge. **91-96:** Thomas Sims Archives. **97:** Wesley & Marilyn Tuttle. **101:** Thomas Sims Archives. **105:** Courtesy Jean Turk Simon (Turk); Manuel Cuevas. **106 & 107:** Thomas Sims Archives. **108:** Manuel Cuevas. **110-116:** Thomas Sims Archives. **124 & 125:** Wesley & Marilyn Tuttle. **126:** Thomas Sims Archives. **128:** Audrey S. Hall.

SOURCE NOTES

All quotes and background from original, previously unpublished and usually multiple interviews conducted between 1993 and 1999 with the author and Gene Autry, Susie Hamblen, Roy Rogers, Dusty Rogers, Cliffie Stone, Marilyn Tuttle, Wesley Tuttle, Buck Owens, Rose Maphis, Doye O'Dell, Eddie Dean, Marty Stuart, Manuel Cuevas, Hank Snow, Rose Clements, Bobbie Cohen, Hank Thompson, Jean Shepard, Thomas Sims, Irwin Simon, Jean Turk Simon, Les "Carrot Top" Anderson, Dottie Ethridge, Roy Rogers Jr., Rose Maddox, and Larry Collins, unless noted below.

Quote from Woody Guthrie in "This Land Is Your Land: the Life and Legacy of Woody Guthrie" exhibit. Organized by the Smithsonian Institution Traveling Exhibition Service and the Woody Guthrie Archives in association with the Center for Folklife and Cultural Heritage, Smithsonian Institution.

Crenshaw, Marshall. Liner notes for *When I Stop Dreaming: the Best of the Louvin Brothers*. New York: Razor & Tie Music, 1995.

Crichton, Kyle. "Rodeo Ben," *Collier's Magazine*, date unknown.

Dellar, Fred, and Thompson, Roy. *The Illustrated Encyclopedia of Country Music*. New York: Harmony Books, 1977.

The El Monte Historical Society Museum, 3150 N. Tyler Avenue, El Monte, California 91732.

Fong-Torres, Ben. *Hickory Wind: The Life and Times of Gram Parsons*. New York: Pocket Books, 1991.

Geller, Greg. Liner notes for *Rockabilly Stars, Vols. 1-3*. New York: Epic Records/CBS (now Sony), 1982.

The Gene Autry Western Heritage Museum, 4700 Western Heritage Way, Los Angeles, California 90027.

Hake, Theodore, and Cauler, Robert. *Sixgun Heroes*. Des Moines, Iowa: Wallace-Homestead Books, 1976.

Hilburn, Robert. *Los Angeles Times*, 1992. His review of Bear Records' Frizzell compendium *His Life, His Music* (rereleased as a 12-CD set, *Life's Like Poetry*) quoted in August 1998 biography on MusicBlvd.com.

Hillbilly Hollywood font designers at testpilotcollective.com

Hopkins, Jerry. "Nudie," *Rolling Stone*: June 28, 1969.

Hurst, Jack. *Nashville's Grand Ole Opry: the First Fifty Years 1925-1975*. New York: Abradale Press, 1989.

Kuntz, Tom. "On the Block: Archives of the King's Rise and Fall." *New York Times*: August 15, 1999.

McDonald, Archie P., Editor. *Shooting Stars: Heroes and Heroines of Western Film*. Bloomington: Indiana University Press, 1987.

Miller, Jim. *The Rolling Stone Illustrated History of Rock & Roll*. New York: Random House/Rolling Stone Press, 1976.

Olesen, Keith. Liner notes for *Maddox Brothers and Rose: 1946-1951, Vols. 1 & 2*. El Cerrito, California: Arhoolie Records, 1976.

Perkins, Carl, and McGee, David. *Go, Cat, Go!* New York: Hyperion, 1996.

Regional History Center, Department of Special Collections, University Library, University of Southern California, Los Angeles, California 90089.

The Roy Rogers & Dale Evans Museum, 15650 Seneca Rd., Victorville, California 92392.

Sayers, Robin. "Lyle Lovett: Man of Style," *In Style*: 1999.

Shelton, Robert. *The Country Music Story: a Picture History of Country and Western Music*. Seacaucus, New Jersey: Castle Books, 1966.

Thomas Sims Archives, P.O. Box 1464, Spring Valley, California 91979. (858) 295-0509.

Titterington, Keith, and Taylor, Jay. "The Les 'Carrot Top' Anderson Story." *Country: Musical Trails Less Traveled Newsletter*, October-November 1990.

Whiteside, Jonny. "The Manifest Destiny of the Maddox Brothers & Rose." *Journal of Country Music*, vol. 2, no. 2, 1986.

Whiteside, Jonny. *Ramblin' Rose: the Life and Career of Rose Maddox*, with an unpublished foreword by Woody Guthrie. Nashville: the Country Music Foundation Press & Vanderbilt University Press, 1997.

Wolfe, Charles K. Liner notes for *Lefty Frizzell: His Life, His Music*. Liner notes for *The Louvin Brothers: Close Harmony*. Bremen, Germany: Bear Family Records.

CDNow.com is a great resource for encapsulated artist biographies, even the more obscure, early country & Western acts discussed in this book. Including: Bush, John. Carl Butler bio, All-Music Guide, CDNow.com, 1999. Eder, Bruce. Jimmy Wakely bio, All-Music Guide, CDNow.com, 1999. Erlewine, Stephen Thomas. Lefty Frizzell bio, All-Music Guide, CDNow.com, 1999.

In researching this history, I also made notes from scrapbooks, mimeographed fans' newsletters, concert bills, and song books, which could not be further identified.

The author wishes to **thank** Audrey Hall, for always helping; Carolyne Fuqua, for the lessons; and Roy Bittan, for his friendship and his music.

I thank the designers Sharon Werner and Sarah Nelson for their understanding of this project and the brilliance they brought to it. Very special thanks to attorney Thomas Sims, whose passion for archiving this era is matched by his generosity. Thanks to Marty Stuart, for the introduction to the wild clothes and the permission to photograph his costume collection. For their contributions to this book and American music, thanks to Larry Collins, Dottie Ethridge, Marilyn and Wesley Tuttle, Les Anderson, Rose Maphis, Rose Maddox, Eddie Dean, Roy Rogers, Dusty Rogers, Gene and Jackie Autry, Rose Clements, Hank Thompson, Buck Owens, Susie Hamblen, Jean Shepard, Doye O'Dell, Manuel Cuevas, Bobbie Cohen, Irwin and Jean Simon, and Bessie Turk. Thanks to Dace Taube at the Regional History Collection at the USC Libraries. I thank Kyle Ericksen for the photographs, the patience, and the long friendship.

Thanks to Bruce Springsteen and the E Street Band, for making me braver. Thanks to Jeff Tweedy of Wilco for playing the Louvins' "Atomic Bomb" one night and making me see a reason to do this book now. And for making me interested in music in the first place, I thank all the young black songwriters, from Harvey Fuqua on, whose songs always shined light into the dark.

For their support of my work, I thank Jessica Kaye, Micheline Rampe, Euan Kerr at Minnesota Public Radio, Jann Wenner, Terry McDonell, Corby Skinner, Bill Borneman, Amy Tharp, Alice Anderson, Barbara DeMarco Barrett, Jean Faraka, Patty Smith, Carol Micale, Marty Keller, Andy Weiner and Lisa McGowan, Liz Sullivan, Pat Lund, and my friends at Weller's Books. And I thank my friends Diane Hayes and Louie Anderson, for their encouragement, and Akili Beckwith, for the prayers.

Debby Bull is the author of a memoir, *Blue Jelly*. *Kirkus Review* called it "enchanting, warm, funny and plump with insight"; *The San Francisco Chronicle* said it was "inventive and refreshingly offbeat...with a gem-like message"; and *The Salt Lake Tribune* called it a "cult classic in the making." She was a writer and editor at *Rolling Stone* magazine. Her writing has also appeared in *Us*, *Interview*, *Smart*, *Premiere*, and other magazines. She lives in Livingston, Montana, and travels the world obsessively.

ABOUT THE AUTHOR

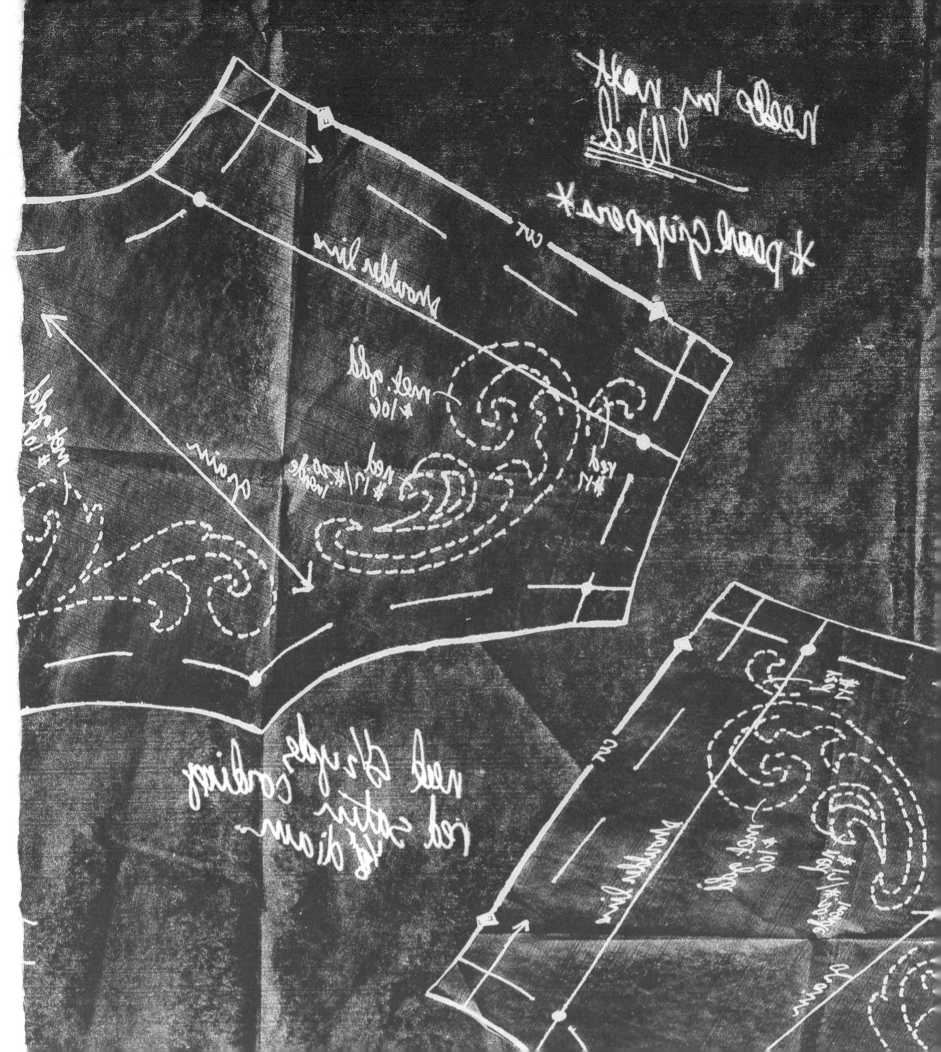

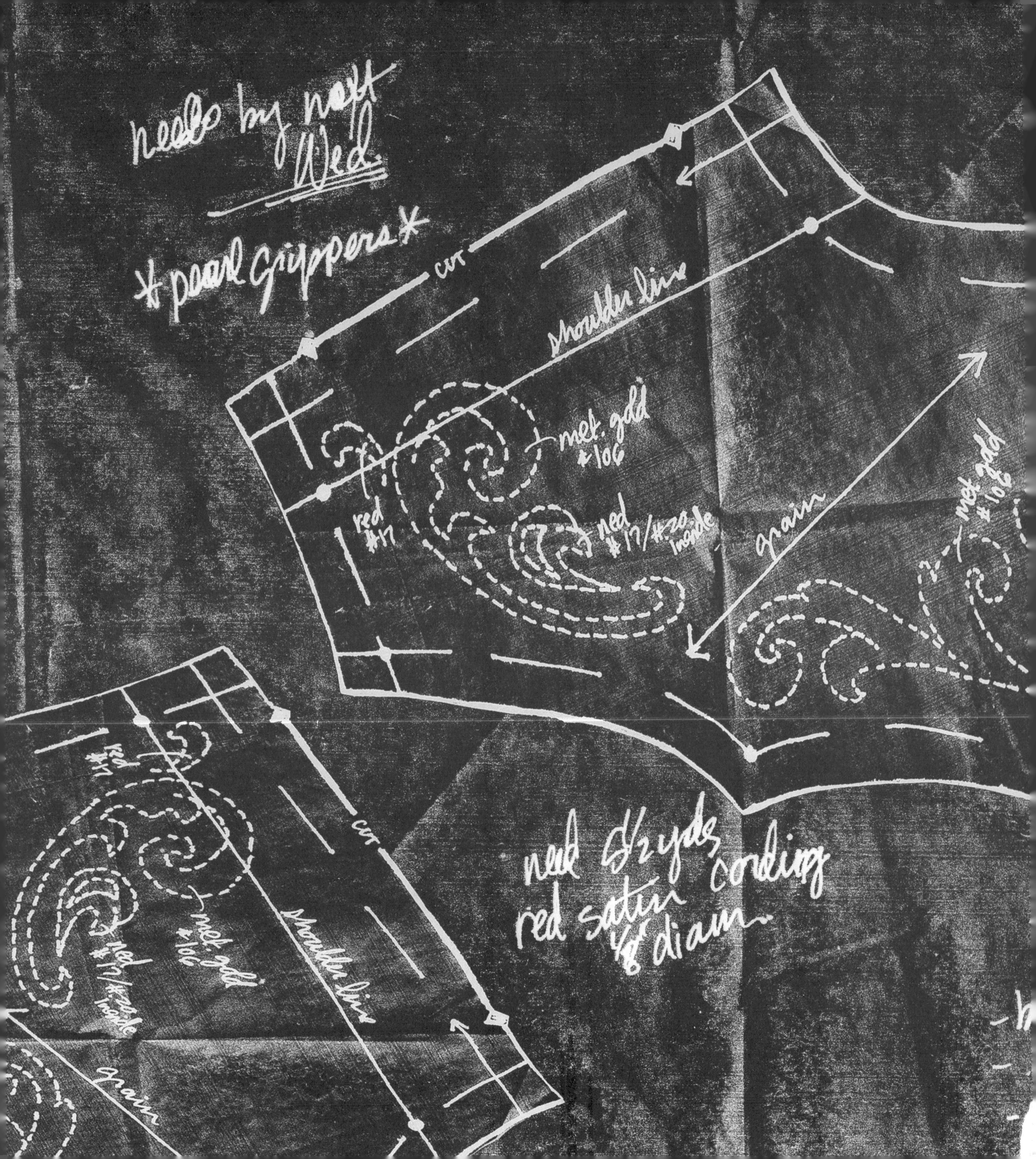
needs by next Wed.
* pearl grippers *
CUT
shoulder line
met. gold #106
red #17
red #17/#20 inside
grain
met. gold #106
red 3 1/2 yds cording red satin 1/8" diam.
red #17
CUT
met. gold #106
shoulder line
red #17/#20 inside
grain